T0022198

About the Author

Erin Newman is a coach, speaker, and author who believes that the magical can also be practical. She lives in Atlanta, Georgia, with her husband, two kiddos, and one adorable dog. Find her online at www.erinnewman.com and in her Facebook group for entrepreneurs, the Spiritual Women Entrepreneurs Collective:

https://www.facebook.com/groups/spiritualentrepreneurscollective.

Erin Newman

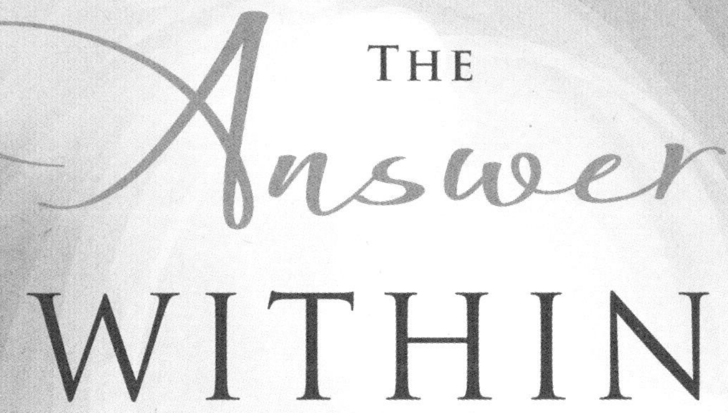

The Answer Within

How to Access Your Spirit Guides for Alignment and Abundance

Llewellyn Publications
Woodbury, Minnesota

First Edition
First Printing, 2023

Cover design by Kevin R. Brown

Llewellyn Publications is a registered trademark of Llewellyn Worldwide Ltd.

Library of Congress Cataloging-in-Publication Data (Pending)
ISBN: 978-0-7387-7482-4

Llewellyn Publications
A Division of Llewellyn Worldwide Ltd.
2143 Wooddale Drive
Woodbury, MN 55125-2989
www.llewellyn.com

Printed in the United States of America

To the Cherokee and Muskogee peoples,
on whose stolen lands I reside.

Contents

Exercises

Chapter 21

Conclusion

Introduction

Sitting in my cubicle day after day, working at a "normal" corporate job, I knew there was something more for me but didn't really think following my dreams was possible. I mean, I had a day job. And a husband. And kids. None of that spiritual stuff was really for me, was it? It was all for someone else, someone who had time to float down the Amazon to hang out with Indigenous healers, wearing a flowy white dress and red leather cowboy boots. Which would have been fairly impractical, but you know, it would've looked good on Instagram.

I couldn't see how to create a life like the ones I read about in all of the books. I mean, these mystics and sages obviously didn't have car payments, mortgages, or kids. Who could tell me how to go from boring suburban mom to that super spiritual woman, the woman who was holding retreats in cool places, hanging out with spiritual peeps, teaching spiritual concepts, and living the life I knew I was meant to live? Surely, someone out there had created a plan for this, right?

Um, no. Spoiler alert: I never found a plan…because there *is* no plan. I managed to find my own way to follow my own sacred and aligned path, and I'm living the life I knew was possible for me while helping others to see that the life they desire is possible for them too. Expanding along that path means continually questioning, and I'm so excited to share the practices I've learned so that you can receive your own answers around your next steps.

We'll be using the practice of journeying as our way to receive guidance from Source and connect to your soul guides. By listening to the simple beat of a drum or music, you'll enter into an altered trance state, similar to a meditation, and then you'll connect with and listen to the answers from your guides. If you're feeling super skeptical right about now, don't worry; I was also super skeptical of this work in the beginning, and I promise we'll make this really accessible both for skeptics and magicians and everyone in between. Also, you'll notice that throughout the book, I'll most often refer to the ineffable energy of the universe with the word "Source," however please choose whichever word feels most resonant for you, whether that's "the All That Is," "God," "Universe," "Goddess," "Creator," "Spirit," or "higher self."

No matter who you are or where you come from, you can learn to access your guides in order to follow your sacred path. And you can utilize that guidance to create a life you love, even if you're still carpooling and fishing Goldfish crackers out of your backseat. You can even follow this path without ever going to Peru, taking Ayahuasca, or buying a single crystal.

This work has its roots in the practices of Indigenous cultures around the world, which are often grouped together under the name of "shamanism," from the Tungus people of Siberia's word *saman*. However, out of respect for the Indigenous people with whom this word is most often identified, including Native Americans in the United States, I don't use the words "shaman" or "Shamanism" to describe my work, nor do I identify as a Shamanic practitioner.

Additionally, it's important to acknowledge my privilege in sharing this work with you. As an upper-middle-class, hetero, cis-gendered, able-bodied White woman, it's much easier for me to step into love and light when I'm not carrying the weight of four hundred years of my ancestors' enslavement and oppression. If you are a woman of color, I see you, and I hope that this work supports you. I don't say this in attempt to be "woke" but in a real acknowledgment of the work still necessary to ensure equity for all people on our planet. To my White friends, if you haven't already, I hope that you'll commit to the hard work of dismantling White supremacy with me in our spiritual circles and spaces.

The practices presented here are shared in the hope that we can all find value in these healing tools. No matter which corner of the world you hail from, your ancestors would have listened to the natural world and their soul guides to receive practical answers to their concerns such as, "Where can we find water for the tribe?" or "Which direction should we walk in?" In our modern world, many of us have concerns that are more like "How do I get my kids to stop eating potato chips?" (That question is entirely hypothetical, of course... not related to the author's personal life at all.)

And while you probably picked up this book because you need help with deeper questions such as, "Which direction do I need to go in life?" or "Just what, seriously, is my sacred path?" please know that this work is meant to be supportive in all aspects of your life. You can take these practices and receive support and guidance for whatever is going on in your very real, very messy life, right now. Yes, even the potato-chip-eating aspects.

Because our work here is focused primarily on alignment and abundance, this book is meant to help you release the fears that might come up when you think about going down a different path or direction in your career, business, or life. You may ask yourself questions such as, "Can I really make money doing *that*?" Short answer: yes. You're going to be able to access your unique answers to those questions and bring the magical back into the practical, allowing you to follow the path of your big dreams and earn money from it too, should you choose.

Whether you absolutely know what your aligned and abundant path looks like or don't have the first clue, you're in exactly the right place. We're going to help you to tune in to your personal power and divine direction, and discover even more of your sacred path in a way that's accessible and easy. You'll be able to truly create a life you love, one that is full of abundance, creativity, joy, and ease—all while in the midst of baking cookies for the bake sale or filing those damn TPS reports.

You're being called to step forward onto your aligned path in an unprecedented time—a time of great uncertainty, misery, and sadness on the planet. The recent events have only shown more of the polarity possible on this physical plane.

However, you're being called to a new existence, one that values the power of connectedness and love above all else. In this new space, you may find your way to an even more expanded sense of self. You might choose to serve others as you walk along your path, or you might not.

Since you're reading this, you're probably someone who chooses to help and serve others, continually learning, teaching, and growing. However, helping others doesn't mean that you must give up your sense of self or in any way denigrate your own wellbeing, energy, or life force. The universe wishes for you to be whole, and when you offer your love and service from a place of wholeness, that in turn allows others to heal.

You must also be sure that you wish to do this work. There will be many times you'll question the path you're on, so you must start with a commitment to yourself and the universe that what you're choosing is the path of the soul, the path of your higher self, the path of God, Source, or universal energy. We're on the path of supporting Mother Earth and all of our brothers and sisters. When you choose this path, many people in your life could fall away, and you could find many situations you need to release. Following your sacred path isn't easy and it's not always clear. Luckily, you'll be given tools that will allow you to walk the path with surety and conviction.

Although the chapters don't necessarily have to be read in order, the first few journeys should be done in sequential order as they do build on each other; i.e., one journey may be necessary to undertake before the next. Please don't feel as though you need to ask every single question in the journeying work with your guides, though; they are meant as prompts for you to explore, so you might only choose one or two as a springboard for your journey. Above all, you're meant to create your own connection to Source and your spirit guides.

Are you ready? Let's begin!

PART 1

Connecting WITH YOUR SPIRIT GUIDES

Chapter 1
SOUL JOURNEYING

When Su came to my latest soul journeying retreat, she was questioning what she wanted to do with her business. She didn't know whether to continue to be a technical writer, which was work she didn't love anymore but was providing her with a steady income, or whether she should move into coaching, work she loved doing. She had lots of questions to ask of her guides!

As Su began journeying during the retreat, she connected to the energy of Butterfly as one of her soul guides. She shared that as soon as she stepped onto the beach, a giant butterfly descended. The butterfly enveloped Su in her wings. "You don't need 'hardcore' protection," Butterfly said, "just a thin sheath, like my wings. They protect you from others' energy." Then she wrapped her legs around Su and they flew together in a powerful experience. Su had other powerful journeys during our time together, and she left the time in the mountains with some clear ideas about her new business venture. She's now thriving as an Intuitive Business Coach.

That's the power of journeying: the ability to receive messages from the energy of the Divine by connecting to your spirit guides. Just as Butterfly became one of Su's new guides, your own guides will show up for you to do this powerful work together, so you can find your own answers to all of the questions you might have about your life.

Spirit guides can take many forms, including power or totem animals, goddesses or gods, ascended masters, star beings, angelic beings, and light beings. You'll notice that I also refer to your spirit guides as helping spirits, power animals, and allies throughout the book; to me, these are all synonyms for the energy of Source. There are also other guides you might choose to work with, including fairies, gnomes, elves, elementals, and representatives from the natural worlds of rocks, crystals, stones, trees, and plants. For the most part, we'll be focused on connecting you to guides that have human qualities, most commonly associated with the upper planes of light.

Before we start diving deep into how to connect to those spirit guides, I'd like to point out a few things to be aware of.

Spiritual Bypassing

Spiritual work is awesome, but don't forget to also take ownership of your human stuff. It's super cool if you can talk to angels and understand the cosmos, but if you're not also working to be kinder and more compassionate, something went wrong somewhere. True seekers are kind, compassionate, and full of laughter for themselves. They take nothing seriously, recognizing our world as an eternal playground. They don't misuse their power or force others to experience life as they do. They hold space for all opinions, even those they disagree with. They don't believe journeying is the only answer or only modality for healing. They show up and take their places fully in this human plane. They don't pretend to be so spiritually aware that they're somehow "better than" the others around them.

When we don't do that hard work of being fully human while also exploring our spiritual side, we can enter a very dark place. We don't get to simply peace out of becoming better human beings simply because we can journey for hours or meditate for an entire weekend. We also don't get to blame the other realms for harm we've caused, in essence saying, "my guides told me I needed to do this thing."

We must still do the hard work of looking into our own patterns and behaviors as possible reasons for the cause of our external problems. Above all, please know that we're all human, so there's no shame here if you recognize yourself in what I'm sharing. This is a continual practice, of course, and most likely a leading edge for many of us. I certainly know this is part of my own work!

Equality and Sovereignty within Your Journeys

If you grew up in a monotheistic religion, you might have received a lot of programming in the "servant/master"–type of relationship with a higher power, where we must seek permission from God for our actions. (Any other recovering Catholics out there?) In this work, however, we're not asking for a god or goddess to tell us what to do. Your spirit guides are not here to force you to do anything, and regardless of which forms your guides might take, you still get to make your own choices with the information provided to you. You have full equality and sovereignty in your journeys and over your own energy.

We humans possess total freedom of choice, even in relation to our soul guides. So even if your spirit allies belong to the pantheon of goddesses, star beings, or ascended masters, we're still operating in partnership. No matter what sort of information, wisdom, and knowledge we bring back from our helping spirits or guides, we still get to choose whether to incorporate that information into our lives or not. We always, always, always have a choice.

If you choose not to follow the advice you were given in a journey because it's too scary or "out there," or just because we forget (hey, we're human), there won't be a "test" later to see if you followed the advice and guidance of your helping spirits. You may still make wrong choices in your life, but you'll never be punished by your helping spirits.

Our guides are not here to serve us or to aid us in a subservient way; they show up for us with the understanding that they are also sovereign beings. My helping spirits have shared that they come to us because we have chosen to answer the call to be light bringers in the world, and they're here to support us in that work. You might want to ask your guides why they show up to support you when we start journeying.

Believing That This Will Be the One Thing That Makes You Happy

As my friend Heather and I walked along a dusty rural road outside of Boulder midway through a training, I tried to put into words my current frustrations: "I thought this training would solve everything. I thought it would make me *happy*." Heather put me in a big bear hug as I cried on her shoulder. "Oh babe," she said, "You put everything into *this* basket?"

As we go down our spiritual paths, all too often we think that the next training, the next modality, the next thing we're exploring is what's going to make us happy, only to find out that happiness is still elusive. I hope this isn't a news flash, but being connected to your helping spirits and spirit guides won't necessarily make you happy, either. Happiness is instead the ongoing practice of continually choosing joy.

The good news is that your helping spirits can help with that ongoing practice of choosing joy and helping you to let go of anything that blocks you from that joy in any moment. Whatever your approach to happiness is, your guides can help you. I'm personally a fan of Buddhism and Eckhart Tolle's approach to happiness, in which we're simply aware of the present moment and continually come back to this moment without judgment, worry, or regret. I find when I'm most unhappy is when I'm not being accepting of a certain situation or person, whether that's my own past or my worries about the future. And of course, we can always work with our guides to shift that energy and bring us back to happiness.

Cultural Appropriation

Journeying practices are part of our shared humanity; our species has been practicing this work since the dawn of humanity. However, many of the current practices used by White people were stolen from Indigenous cultures all over the world, period. Full Stop. We therefore need to ask whether White people have any right at all to practice shamanism or journeying. Is there any place at all for ethical, conscious, White shamans?

As mentioned in the introduction, I land personally on no longer using the words "shaman" or "Shamanism" to define my work. Most often, when people use the word "shaman," they are imagining the healers and medicine people of the Indigenous peoples of the United States, and I don't wish to capitalize on an association, real or perceived, with the beautiful healers who do this work on behalf of their people.

At the same time, the more people who are open to connecting to Source, welcoming in the light, and respecting and communing with nature, the better. My personal guidance from my guides around this question has been to continue to share this work and show up as a White woman who can perhaps guide others into this work without appropriating the words, ceremonies, and powerful traditions from other cultures and communities.

White people must continue to find ways to navigate a world in which White Europeans have taken so much from so many peoples. We have a responsibility to be aware of where our practices come from and to not appropriate specific religious symbols, ceremonies, and words from Indigenous people or the First People of the Americas for usage in White ceremonies without express permission or training in that lineage. This includes things like the word "smudging," a term specifically used by Indigenous cultures. We have a huge responsibility to look into our own internalized racism both regarding our Black sisters and brothers and to the Indigenous communities who were here in what would come to be called the Americas long before us.

For my White friends, here are some ideas for offering support to people of color and Native Americans: we can show up and support them as they lead circles, we can see them as spiritual teachers and leaders, and we can offer our platforms for them to lead and teach us. We can seek ways to learn from other cultures when we are invited. We can make sure that the circles we lead are inclusive and safe. We can make a pledge on our websites to support antiracism and name our personal commitments there. We must do the painful work of dismantling our own systemic racism and pay for that work. We can give money to support Indigenous cultures and their preservation. We can give over our spaces, homes, and offices to non-White teachers for their use at no cost. We can be silent when our black and brown friends are speaking, and we can be vocal when we see injustices perpetuated by White people. We can notice where we have not done these things in the past and make amends now.

All of us who choose to undertake a spiritual path should choose to have these deeper conversations, to show up and do this powerful work of looking at our own preconceived notions, and if you are White, to be willing to listen to the voices of those who haven't had the same privileges of skin color. There will not be an easy path forward here, and I don't claim any answers; I simply know that we must look into our own internalized prejudices and to continue to see spiritual communities as a place where these conversations also need to happen.

You might choose to journal your answers to the following questions:

- What are some ways I can be more inclusive?
- Where are spaces that I can learn from other cultures?
- What are some of the biases and racism that I've held onto in the spiritual community?
- I can best support other cultures by . . . .
- What does sovereignty mean to me?
- Where is my ego showing up as I explore my spirit guidance?

Chapter 2
Discovering Your Spirit Guides

Experiencing your guides for the first time will most likely be one of the most beautiful and powerful experiences of your life. The reason receiving guidance from your guides is so powerful and helpful is not just because we're entering a meditative state (though that alone confers so many health benefits); the power comes from entering a *dynamic conversation* to facilitate healing and guidance on a deeper level of our minds. Through journeying to our guides, we're creating a place where our rational, logic-minded brain is temporarily relegated to the back seat, allowing us to pick up on answers that come from the greater mind. As you drop into either alpha or theta brain waves in a journey, you'll be able to access a state of consciousness more powerful than just logic, a place where Einstein drew his ideas from, perhaps even a place where you might find some answers to that potato chip question.

Questioning Whether This Work Is Real

I can almost guarantee that as soon as you start journeying, you'll be asking, "Are these guides really there? Am I just imagining this? Am I doing this right?" Every person I've ever known from a Western background who enters this work has asked themselves the exact same questions. Perhaps it's possible to ask yourself this question instead: is what I'm being shown more beautiful, accurate, and powerful than anything my conscious mind could have come up with? For instance, some of the lessons I've been given in my journeys are to relax, to laugh more, to love my children and husband more, to spend more time in nature, to be an advocate for those who don't feel empowered, to offer this work to others in a bigger way, to release anger at friends and family, to welcome more abundance into my life, pursue my life purpose, and discover more of the gifts and magic I bring to this world. And these are not usually just words that my guides share with me but instead powerful images and scenes that allow my subconscious mind to rapidly assimilate the teachings. These are such powerful lessons; I no longer doubt the power of the connection to the unseen realms.

Another question that often comes up is, "Is my subconscious mind just coming up with answers?" Maybe! However, even if the message is "only" coming from your subconscious mind, isn't your mind also a part of Source energy? If we know that our mind *is* part of the energy of the Divine, we can more readily accept that whatever is showing up for us—whether "imagined" or a "true" message from our helping spirits—is exactly what's most needed for us to know in that moment.

The more you journey and connect to your soul guides and allow more of what you see and experience to be valid, the easier it becomes to accept that the guidance you're receiving is "real." Simply be accepting of your rational mind and know that those questions will most likely arise, and at the same time, allow the journey to unfold. What I've found in years of hosting workshops and retreats is that most people are able to access their guides and allies *if* they can drop the left-brain mind chatter. We all have equal access to the Divine or Source energy; no one is gifted with more connection ability than anyone else.

The good news is that you don't have to believe fully in this work to experience healing and transformation. You can step into this work with full skepticism and still experience the benefits of expansion and light in your soul, mind, and physical body. It all starts with learning the steps to experiencing rich and full journeys and understanding how to create connections with your soul guides that are stable and lasting. Doing so allows you to ask questions and be supported with whatever's most concerning you right now.

Different Ways of Receiving Wisdom

We all see differently. Some find that connecting with their guides is more of a felt sense or a sensing of the energy, and others receive auditory messages very clearly. The more you are able to tell yourself that the way that your guides are showing up for you is exactly the way they "should" show up, the more deeply you will be able to drop into connection with your guides.

The spirit guides we'll be working with may speak to us in many ways, both during the journey as well as in ordinary reality, including the following:

- Claircognizant: we receive the information as "drops" or "pings" (aka "downloads")
- Clairaudient: we hear
- Clairvoyant: we see
- Clairolfactant: we smell
- Clairsentient: we feel
- Another combination thereof

All these methods are equally valid; all healers process and receive their guidance in different ways, and sometimes that way of processing changes even within the same journey. You may be feeling a tug to give credence to one type of sensing than another, usually clairvoyance, or "seeing stuff" in your journeys, however any way in which you're given the information can be valid and true and supportive if you allow it to be.

Connecting to Specific Spirit Guides

For doing any kind of work in this book, you'll be asked to connect with a particular guide around that specific concern or question. For instance, if you are most concerned right now with your health, you could ask the spirit realm to show you a guide for your health. The process for connecting to any of your guides is pretty much the same as what you just experienced with connecting to your higher self. You'll want to drop into a very relaxed state and then ask to connect with a guide for that particular concern or area of your life.

Connecting with your guides requires practice; journeying isn't going to be something you can do just once and expect your whole life to change. In the same way that you wouldn't expect your entire physique to change with one trip to the gym even if you worked out really hard, we can't expect that our entire spiritual life will change with one journey. That said, miracles often happen!

Even after you've been receiving guidance for a while, you might still ignore it. For instance, I was recently washing a load of cold laundry and heard a whisper from my guides: *don't turn on the wash yet*. Like any sane and rational person, I ignored the voice. I had to get the laundry done, damn it! This was Tuesday, my laundry day!

Then I went out to run errands, and realized my period had arrived, which decided to be very heavy. In addition to the car seat, my favorite jeans needed to be cleaned immediately. They could have nicely gone into that wash that I'd already done.

Your helping spirits will help with all aspects of your life, if you allow them to. You live on this physical plane, and your helping spirits are here to help with your human experience.

Is Having Multiple Guides Necessary?

You might work with only one guide initially. And as you choose to deepen into this work, you might find that different guides will often offer different perspectives and guidance on the same issue, and you can journey to more than one guide within one journey and receive an even deeper layer of wisdom, support, and healing.

For instance, when I have something going on in my business, I usually journey to both my abundance guide and the guide for my business and we examine various programs and offers and tune into the energy behind those offers to see if both the pricing and the marketing are aligned for me and my ideal clients. My business guide also helps me create names for my programs, books, and offers, so they're definitely powerful allies to have. And even when it's related to business, the guidance I receive most often is to be in connection with the land and nature even more; to simply be without "efforting" quite so much; and to simply feel into the energy required to support a group, person, or program.

Your guides can also easily help you to shift the energy around a problem or concern with another person in your business or career. You'll find that when you shift the energy behind the problem, you don't require nearly as much energy in the "real world" for the problem to go away, often entirely of its own accord. This guidance is always available to you at any moment. You don't need to wait for a time to journey or even close your eyes—you're able to access the wisdom of your inner power and guidance whenever you want. Simply ask for the highest wisdom to flow through you and it will be done.

Most of us aren't willing to pause to take the moment to reconnect with our soul guidance. We allow our lizard brain to take over and react with fear, which is normal. It would be really hard for anyone to simply wake up and be rid of a lifetime of conditioning, all of which was created to keep you safe as a child. Instead, choose a simple acknowledgment of where you are and what you are being called to do in this moment: become a better version of yourself (even as opposed to who you were five minutes ago) and allow yourself the patience of a loving mother offering unconditional love to a child. Your guides and the infinite All-That-Is see you through the eyes of unconditional love. When you can begin to allow that unconditional love to envelop you, wrap you in its arms and hold you with the light of the universe, you'll receive the insights you've been seeking. All it takes is this moment of awareness leading to the next. You've already done so much and are ready for more. You're ready to be called into the love that Source has for you and for that love to be in each of your present moments.

If your current struggles are within your vocation or business, that's also where you're being called to share more love—with yourself, your peers, your colleagues, your boss, your employees, the people around you. Sharing love is the path to resolving the worry and stress and creating more abundance.

Continue to deepen your experience of this unconditional love and acceptance of what is. Continue to expand into more by claiming what is being shown. Know that it is already yours, as you are worthy of all that you can see. Ask your guides for the answers to the "how" and see what might be revealed there.

Even if you feel like you're not great at meditation, you can still start a journeying practice. Some people find journeying much easier than meditation. In journeying, you aren't trying to release all of your thoughts. Instead, you're seeking specific guidance and connection with your guides.

If you get stuck and start feeling like you're not "seeing" something in your journeys, allow your imagination to take over. Many cultures don't make as much of a distinction between what is real and what is imagined as Western cultures do. So when you feel a sense that you're not getting a message, allow yourself to imagine that soul guide appearing before you and imagining what they might share or offer in response. You might have heard it in metaphysical teachings that your imagination is the gateway to reality. You get to create your own reality through the power of your mind. If and when you feel stuck or lost in a journey, simply imagine what you would like to see. Let go of needing to know whether it's your imagination or an actual message from Source.

Another way to increase your power of perception in your journeys is to increase the intensity of what you're already experiencing. Ask yourself: what else you can you sense, feel, or smell in your journey? If you're able to see even a little bit of color in your journeys, perhaps you can intensify the color you're seeing, as if you were turning up a dial. The same goes with your other senses: can you imagine turning up the dial on the sounds you're hearing, the feeling of your body in the journey?

Asking the Right Questions in Your Journeys

The stone beings that came to me during a journey in Colorado were incredibly powerful. They represented the energy of the land on which I was journeying, and they were there to support me in any work I did with the land. However, I had to learn how to work with them. And for someone who's a recovering type-A personality, they operated at the level of stone—changing over eons, shaped by the earth's natural forces. They moved slowly and answered my questions slowly. My task was to ask questions they could respond to in their way, therefore allowing me to tune into their frequency and co-create a healing space for the work we were supposed to do together.

The idea of coherency is one that needs to be named as you begin to ask questions of your guides and spirit animals. We are not asked to be "high vibe" all the time. Instead, we are asked to become more coherent with our energetic frequency. We want our brain wave patterns and the light waves we're emitting to become steadier. Coherency also applies to the questions we're asking. Our guides don't do well with vague questions. To be more accurate, our guides don't have the same concepts of "good" and "bad" as we humans do. For instance, something that we might see as a relatively negative outcome to a situation such as losing your job and ending up sleeping your car is on a soul level, really neither good nor bad. It simply is what it is: a learning experience for you, the human, to have while you're here on this earth.

Even things that we would think that most of us would believe to be bad, such as contracting a disease, becoming ill, or even dying are again not given measurement or judgment from the perspective of our soul guides. If our soul mission on this earth is to learn and grow and expand, then all of those experiences would still be contributing to our soul's path.

While you don't need to experience any of the things we would call "negative," as you begin to ask important life questions, you'll want to formulate your questions in an open-ended way to allow your helping spirits to show you different perspectives and possible outcomes. For instance, one question you can always ask of your helping spirits is, "Could you please show me different perspectives around _______ situation?" You might also choose to ask the question, "Could you please show me what I might know around ______ situation?"

You'll also start to notice that different guides and beings have different ways of responding to your questions. Some might simply show you the answers. Others might show themselves only in times of healing work. Remember that none of these ways of seeing are wrong, and none of the ways that our helping spirits answer our questions are wrong or right, either. Your mission is to trust the answers in whichever ways they're shown.

One other important note in formulating questions is that you begin to trust a process where the question itself becomes irrelevant. Sometimes you might journey to work with a certain animal or helping spirit and not have a specific question at all but just know that if something feels off in that specific aspect of your life, the helping spirit or ally who can most help will show up for you.

Sometimes I'll simply journey without a specific purpose at all, and the helping spirit who most has something to share with me appears and then offers an insight, a healing, or guidance around a particular area of my life. For instance, Cardinal brings me messages around my work with my oldest son and offers a feeling of continual healing and softening so that I can continue to offer unconditional love, even when I'm feeling anything *but* unconditional love for my teen.

As you become more adept at asking questions and receiving answers, you might also like to begin journeying for others in order to receive answers. Although I go into a little more detail on this in later chapters, I'll say here that it's always important to first have permission for this work, even if you're doing it on behalf of one of your children, perhaps *especially* for our kids. You can use the questions in the list that follows to receive guidance for friends and clients. As you share the guidance with the other person, it's important to let go of any attachment to ego—simply share the information as it was presented to you in a way that would be most healing and supportive to them.

Here are open-ended questions and statements you can use when asking for the help of your spirits. As you deepen into your connection to your helping spirits over the next chapters, you can always return to these:

- Please show me what can be known about ________ situation.
- Please offer me healing around ________ situation.
- What perspective can be shown here?
- If I were to take X decision, what possible outcomes can be known?

JOURNEYING WORK

Connect with Your Higher Self

First, find a quiet and dark place for journeying. You might sit or lie down as you would for meditation, though I find I journey best while lying down. You could also use an eye mask if it helps you drop more deeply into an altered state. Next, play a recording of a drumbeat or theta waves music, and allow yourself to drop into a very deep meditative state. Once you have done so, ask to meet with your higher self. You might have done this in a meditation before, but it's important to firmly establish this connection to your higher self before any further journeying, even if only for a few seconds.

Connecting with your higher self will become one of the main practices that you'll return to again and again. The more you practice the connection, the more you'll find that you're able to tune in at any time for guidance and connection, even while sitting in a coffee shop. Connecting to your higher self before journeying also ensures we are operating from that place of the highest good for self and others.

You'll know that you're actually connected when you feel a sense of peace and lightness; when your higher self offers guidance, it should feel gentle and soft, never a harsh voice that uses the words "should" or "must." Remember that there will not be a test, and there's no getting it right. Simply allow. Ready? Let's do it!

Step One: Turn on a drumbeat or theta waves music on your phone or computer. For drumming, I personally like just a simple drumbeat without any additions like birdsong or chanting, but some people prefer nature sounds or other sounds in the background. What's most important is that the recording is three to four drumbeats per second.

Step Two: Lie down on the ground (my favorite way to journey), or in a chair if you have problems getting up and down. Place an eye mask or even a towel over your eyes. It's also best if the room is as dark as possible, but with the eye mask, you'll be able to achieve a dark enough state.

Step Three: Connect with the ground and Mother Earth, breathing in to where your body is lying on the ground. This helps you to enter the altered trance state necessary for a journey.

Step Four: Ask to connect with your higher self. After connecting with your higher self in whichever form is taken, you could ask for a ritual or small ceremony that will initiate you into this work of connecting to your soul guides and your sacred path.

Once you feel that connection to your higher self (which may be only a felt sense, a very vivid image, or some other way of experiencing your higher self), you might choose to ask your higher self these questions or try the following:

- "How can I connect with you when I am not journeying? Is there a talisman, stance, mindset, or way of seeing that will allow me to connect in ordinary reality?" The answer might be a particular mudra, a symbol, or an actual physical item such as a rock or crystal.

- Ask to merge with your higher self. Really step into the presence of your higher self and become your higher self. How does this feel? What do you sense?
- Ask for a healing and/or attunement to your higher self. There are no right or wrong answers as to what that might look like.
- Ask how you can be more connected to this higher self at all times. How does your higher self "see" things differently around you? The answer might be exploring your connection to your body, including chronic pain, illness, health, weight. It could be in connection to your relationships with family members, partners, friends, coworkers. You could be asked to explore your responsibilities, job functions, duties, and your relationship with the unseen world, the environment, the current political situation, with death and the afterlife, and with your role as a healer.

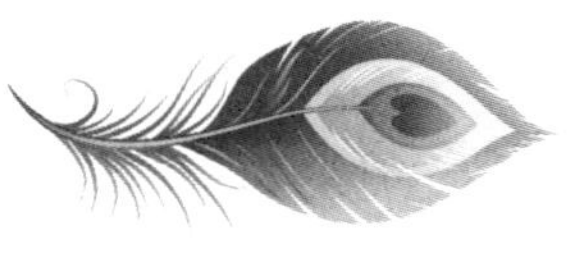

Chapter 3

Connecting to a Body Protector and Gatekeeper

Connecting with your guides is not the only way to heal your life, nor is it the only way to find your inner power and follow your soul. However, it is one way to help you to explore what is right and true for you and is really powerful work! But you won't be able to experience any of that without doing the actual journeys.

The journeys in this chapter are meant to introduce you to guides who will set the sacred container for your journey, to help you to recognize the sacred aspects of your journey, and to offer protection as your soul travels. Just a little thing, right? I highly encourage you to spend time with these important guides.

Journeying to the Gatekeeper

Your gatekeeper is the window through which the other realms become visible and a helper who allows the journey to unfold. They can give structure to your journey; they might provide insights as to what is needed or expected in a particular journey, and they can serve as a regulator of the journey's power and permeability. Checking in with a gatekeeper before a journey will also allow you to have more powerful journeys and be supported as you journey between the realms in an even more expansive way. Your gatekeeper is also there for protection. In times when you "shouldn't" be journeying (e.g., if your intention isn't yet clear or it's simply not a propitious time), working with your gatekeeper can also help bring clarity to your journeys. Translation: your gatekeeper might simply say, "Not a good time, friend. Come back later."

As we do with all our journeys to new helping spirts, we'll start by asking for a name. Then we'll ask about the particular gifts and magic that they bring to you, in addition to any offerings or rituals that might be important to stay in connection with the gatekeeper. And while that sounds like a lot, you can do it all in a fifteen-minute journey!

Since this is a gatekeeper, you'll ask what signs and symbols they will use to tell you when it's safe or appropriate for you to journey on a particular day. My gatekeeper simply shakes his head, but yours might use other words, symbols, or gestures.

Although we always have the choice on how to proceed and whether to follow the gatekeeper's wisdom, our gatekeeper's role is to show us whether a particular journey should be undertaken, so it's probably a good thing to respect whatever your gatekeeper is saying. You won't always know why your gatekeeper is telling you that it's not a good time to journey. Sometimes, I will ask additional clarifying questions such as, "Is there anything I need to do before entering?" and might be given the advice to connect with my higher self for an extended period before journeying. Sometimes my gatekeeper then says, "Okay, cool, come on in," and other times it's still a no—and I always respect that. You have free will, *and* you also might want to honor the role and the power of the gatekeeper before attempting to journey.

Protecting Yourself in Your Journeys

When I first encountered my body protector, I was kind of weirded out. She's an octopus, and her method of protecting me was to cover me in slime. (Remember Slimer from Ghostbusters? Yeah, just like that.) I was not happy. I wanted a "cooler" body protector, like a wolf or a cobra or something more badass ... or even a helping spirit who wasn't going to cover me in slime.

But as we undertook a few journeys together, she showed me how wonderfully amazing octopuses are in all their brilliant wisdom and abilities. She shared a beautiful vision of our ancient ancestors emerging from the depths of the ocean, and she has also taught me about motherhood and my role as a journeying practitioner within this modern world. She showed me a beautiful process for sinking into her embrace at the beginning of each of our journeys, and to this day she continues to provide stability, grounding, and beautiful connection. So maybe an octopus isn't the "coolest," but she's just right for me.

The word "protection" might imply that there are things you will need to be protected from while doing this work. If you believe that to be true, it is. I choose to believe the work I do is always held in the light, and I also enjoy having a relationship with my body protector. She's been very supportive when I'm exploring past lives, for instance. You can create your own relationship with your body protector, the helping spirit or guide who is available to set boundaries and sacred intentions as your soul travels.

Traditionally, a body protector will protect the physical body of the person taking the journey as their soul travels to other realms. The body protector is also an essential helper for remaining grounded during journeys.

All these relationships with your allies are powerful in and of themselves. They are available to offer answers to your questions about each aspect of your journey and will always offer a perspective and shift in thinking that will create more openness and expansiveness in your spiritual work and personal life. We are seeking the power of restorative, unconditional love in our connections with these allies. When you seek out your body protector with the journeys at the end of this chapter, spend some time in their presence. Understand their beautiful ways of seeing and ask yourself: how are they important to your journeying? What magic do they bring to you? What magic do you offer to them? What can they share for you, right now, today, that will be of benefit to you and to those around you?

And also, stop searching for meanings on the internet! I know you're going to want to look up your body protector on the internet. But maybe, just maybe … don't. Instead of searching "What does this spirit animal mean?" from a website, you can simply ask your guides: What do you symbolize for me? What do you intend for me to see? Why are you here for me? And how can we deepen into that connection?

Once you've experienced the power of connecting to your guides, you'll have all the tools you need to deepen into your sacred path at hand, and there is no better guide for this work than your personal helping spirits and allies. When you have a question, you can turn to an ally or guide at each turning point and simply ask them about the meaning or meanings behind something. They *will* answer.

In the journeys that follow, you will also be asking for your unique way for your body protector to offer their ways of protection and guidance at the start of each one. (Also, you might receive your own sliming. It's fun, I promise!)

Your body protector might also function as a container to hold your earthly worries and concerns as you journey. When you connect with your body protector, you can release fears and thoughts that might hold you back from entering the journeying space, and you might opt to make this connection immediately after your gatekeeper has opened the gates for you.

JOURNEYING WORK
Connect with Your Gatekeeper

Find your journeying space, ask to be connected to your gatekeeper, and then explore what your gatekeeper can help you with in your journeys. It might be a simple check-in, lasting only a few seconds where you acknowledge your body protector's presence, or there might be a longer process you are asked to complete first. You'll get those answers by asking questions of your body protector in your journeys, such as the following:

- Please show me what it looks like when the gates are fully open. (There may be a specific word or symbol or feeling shown here.)
- Can you please show me what it looks like/feels like when my gates are fully closed? (There may be a word or symbol or feeling shown here.)
- Please show me ways in which we can work together.
- What magic do you bring?
- What gifts do you bring?
- How might I honor you?
- Is there anything you need in the way of an offering or ceremony?
- How will I know when we are connected? What will that look like?
- Is there anything that you would ask of me? Are there ways in which I can honor you?

A helping spirit may ask you to "dance" the spirit, or offer a ceremony or make an offering of some kind. Sometimes our power animals and helping spirits like to simply experience the world through us. As always, the "what" and "how" don't seem quite as important as the intention. Remember too that you always have a choice of whether to honor the request or not.

JOURNEYING WORK

Connect to Your Body Protector

Much like your gatekeeper, connecting with your body protector can be a powerful process. Find your journeying space and then ask to be connected with a body protector.

- Is there a symbol, stance, talisman that allows us to connect, both before journeying and in ordinary reality?
- How can I be in partnership with you?
- What rituals, ceremonies, and/or routines, will help me to grow in partnership with you?
- How might I honor you?
- What magic do you bring?
- How will I know when we are connected? What will that look like?

Part 2

Alignment

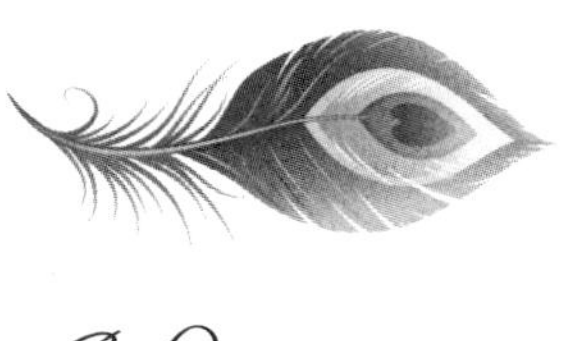

Chapter 4
Discovering Your Soul Path

Many of us turned to spiritual work with the hope that at some point, we would discover our soul's purpose. After that, our entire life would change: money would rain down from the sky, life would be easy and light, and our Instagram posts would be all sunshine and rainbows. Maybe you've even bought about a million books that promise to help you discover that purpose, and maybe you even read them. But at some point, you went back to real life. You've got bills to pay, and real life is unfolding all around you. You aren't even sure you would know your purpose if it jumped out of that bin of mismatched socks and bit you on the nose.

Now you're saying, "Yeah, lady, so just help me actually find my soul purpose." Okay, I will! Ready? Your soul's purpose is to learn and grow and discover all that you can during this one beautiful life, while experiencing joy and helping others.

Consider whether you could perhaps let go of the need to define one specific soul purpose for your life. Instead, let's help you get comfortable with expanding along your unique and aligned sacred path, day by day and minute by minute. The use of the word "path" is deliberate; perhaps there is no destination or end to this path, and you are instead following what lights you up every day and over the course of the years.

As I write this, we are in the middle of the COVID-19 pandemic and a lockdown. Fear and stress are currently at epic levels, and it's been tough to fully show up as myself. I return to my helping spirits again and again for support along my path. Sometimes, that support might look like my helping spirits holding me in a healing posture. Other times, it takes the form of a more active process to transmute pain or anger. And still at other times, support takes the form of asking specific questions and receiving guidance and answers.

The ability to step into this other realm even for a few moments is deeply restorative. Over and over, my helping spirits show me that the sacred path is always a place of expansion, even as we live through "unprecedented times."

The great news is that you can find a helping spirt or ally for any healing work you're doing in your life, including an exploration of your soul path. For example, you could look for a helping spirit to assist you with physical pain, in your relationship to your children or spouse, or even for a new creative project like a book or artwork. These helping spirits might serve specific roles or they may be generalists who have come to help with many different aspects of your life and spiritual work.

Since we're exploring how to expand along on your sacred path here, though, we want to establish a relationship or connection to a helping spirit who can help you with that specific aim. We start as we would with any relationship: getting to know them. We'll be asking what there is to know about your helping spirit, and how it's possible to stay in connection.

Enter the journey by connecting first to your higher self, then your gatekeeper, and then your body protector. Next, set your intention to meet with a specific helping spirit who can support you as you travel your sacred path. Even if this helping spirit isn't totally clear to you and you only see glimpses or aspects, simply rest in the knowledge that your sense of the helping spirit is true.

This helping spirit will be a powerful ally throughout the rest of this book. The great thing about learning how to connect with an ally is that you'll be able to connect with a helping spirit for any kind of question or work you choose (yep, even that "help me stop eating potato chips" ally).

As you create a relationship with this specific helping spirit, you might be asking yourself again, "Is this really working? Are these helping spirits really talking to me?" As before, take a deep breath, allow your rational mind to form all these questions, and then ask your new helping spirit about anything that remains unclear to you. You don't need to do research on the internet about your helping spirit—instead, ask your helping spirits themselves! You are empowered to create relationships with these helping spirits independent of any book, teaching, or internet guru.

You might find that the power animal or ally you encounter doesn't match your expectations. You might have wished for something "cooler" as a helping spirit or ally. That doesn't make you less spiritual—it simply makes you human. You have an ego. It's okay. And you are absolutely allowed to open up that dialogue with your helping spirit and ask them why a specific ally showed up for you, and to help you to understand your personal beliefs about what a helping spirit or power animal "should" look like. You are even allowed to question, whine, and bemoan this work, and then to come back to the magic, whenever you choose.

JOURNEYING WORK

Connect to a Spirit Guide for Your Sacred Path

We're going to ask to meet with a helping spirit, power animal, or ally here specifically to help you to follow your sacred path and ask for an attunement to their energy.

We'll be connecting with your power animal or guide for your aligned path throughout the book, so it's important to create this connection before moving forward. And remember, no need to force yourself to "see" your guide here; simply allow and yes, imagine it, if it still feels hard.

Lie down and take a few deep breaths. Really sense your body lying down. In order to access this world, you'll want to picture a place in your mind that you've visited in ordinary reality in which you can go beneath the earth. It could be a well, an ocean, a river, the root system of a tree, a cave, or a cavern.

Picture that place in your mind's eye. Connect with your higher self, then your gatekeeper, and then your body protector. Then, allow yourself to enter the earth. You might only sense darkness for a moment. Allow all your senses to open, and begin to explore the lower world with all of your senses.

Then, ask to meet with this helping spirit for your sacred path work. Get to know your helping spirit in a gentle way by being in their presence at first, and then, over the course of two or more journeys, you might like to ask the following or similar:

- Why are you here for me? What sorts of things are you here to help me with?
- What gifts, magic, medicine do you bring?

- How can I be in partnership with you?
- What rituals, ceremonies, routines, will help me to grow in partnership with you?
- Are there ways for me to honor you?

Chapter 5

NAMING YOUR SACRED PATH

Most of us spend so much time seeking that one thing that will define our lives instead. So, if after the last chapter, you still think, "Yeah, but seriously, lady, I just need to know what my soul purpose really *is*, and more importantly, I need to find the words to define it," then this chapter is meant to give you a little bit of definition, while at the same time asking you to simply step forward along that sacred path, perhaps without yet knowing exactly what your big, bold work is called.

You don't have to put yourself in a box of any kind, and yet we all have a very human desire to give names to things. We have to find a balance here between the spirit world and the world of humans. And we can find that balance simply by getting clear on the direction we want to go in.

If you're thinking, "But I don't even know the direction! I don't even know which step to take," here's some tough love: you actually *do* know in which direction you would like to head; it's fear that stops you, fears that say, "You can't do that. That's not okay. That's not acceptable." Societal conditioning blocks many of us from allowing Source to provide us with the next steps to take. That doesn't mean you won't be able to get some clear insights and perhaps even a clear definition for your sacred work. For the most part, the work you're supposed to be doing… is probably what you are already doing. You're probably sharing and serving others in the capacity you want to but maybe in a slightly different arena, smaller scale, or a different way than what's totally ideal for you. And when you let go of the fear, you will most likely be able to access more clarity and definition along your sacred path.

Of course, following your sacred path is a continual unfolding; we're never fully done, and as soon as we feel like we've figured it all out, things shift and change again, and we're once again redefining who we are and the work we do. We're continually stepping into the flow of the river that is our sacred path, allowing ourselves to become open to the messages that spirit is showing us over and over again.

Most of us crave assurance and clarity, but following a sacred path means continually being in a state of not-knowing-ness. Release any idea about how things will play out; only take the next step and then the next after that.

Release the pressure on yourself to have everything figured out right now along with the belief that naming it will assure you of its success. The truth is that there are no assurances. No one can promise you that your life's path will be "successful." Instead, you have to step out into the unknown, continually.

But you want more details about the work you want to do in this world, not just some advice about stepping into the void, right? So let's do that. We start with the **Ideal Life Intention** exercise to give you some clarity. It is a deceptively simple exercise (and even if you've done it before, let's do it again) that I do in a different form about once a week and encourage my clients to do often.

Ideal Life Intention

First, grab a pen and journal. Then take a few deep breaths, close your eyes, inhale into your heart center, and then imagine it's five years in the future, and you're talking about your amazing life with a friend. Go through each area of your life and name everything amazing that's happened, including all the experiences you've been having in this ideal world. Hold nothing back—really sink into how juicy all of this ideal life feels for you. Write it all down, perhaps including answers to some of the following questions:

- What are you doing? Who are you speaking with in this ideal world?
- What types of activities are you doing or enjoying?
- How are your relationships with family and friends? What are you enjoying together?
- What does your bank account look like?
- What is your living situation? Describe the house or apartment and its environment. Are you near a beach, water, mountains, in a city, etc.?
- What does your work situation look like? How many hours per week are you working? Do you have a team of helpers, and if so, what are they doing?
- Do you have more childcare / household care / lawn-care / stylists / web designers ... etc.?
- What does your health look like in this ideal world?
- How would you ideally be spending your time?
- What would your ideal work life look like?
- When would you wake up? And when would you go to work?
- What would you be doing during your ideal day? For most of us, that list probably doesn't include the cooking, cleaning, and shopping.

And, just in case you get stalled for inspiration, let's toss out a few other ideas for your juiciest, most ideal life ever:

Would you also . . .

- Take Fridays off?
- Only work ten hours per week?
- Meet the kids for lunch once per week?
- Have a regular date night with your spouse, partner, and/or friends?
- Hire that assistant? Get more help in your business?
- Hire someone to do the laundry, the yard work, some babysitting?

Ideal Life Intention Variation

If you're having a hard time with writing down the things you really want, here's another variation. Sometimes it's easier to name things that we don't want in our lives. Most of us can easily name the things that are bugging us, right? So if that's where you find yourself, try this exercise instead.

Fold a piece of paper in half length-wise. On the left-hand side, list all the things you don't want in your life. Here are a few of mine, just to get you thinking:

- I don't want to do laundry anymore.
- I don't want to cook anymore.
- I don't want to listen to whiny children.

- I don't want to have to tell people what having a coach is, or what having a mindset coach is like.
- I don't want a beach house.

Then we'll use the right half of the paper to create the list of things you truly desire. Again, I'm listing a few of mine for inspiration:

- A beautiful mountain home for retreats and workshops.
- A place out west.
- Time in the mornings for my writing and meditation.
- A business that allows me to travel to Europe and cool places in the US for retreats, workshops, and speaking engagements.

Got some great answers? Cool. Maybe even some things you hadn't thought of before? Awesome. At this point, fear might start to kick in; you might start to tell yourself that none of those things are actually possible or perhaps not possible for you specifically. One of the most important thing you can do for yourself for any kind of personal change is simply taking baby steps toward that dream life. One question I'm always asking my clients is, "How can you get some of that life right now? How can you step into that life just a little bit right now?" As you incrementally upgrade your life, bit by bit, you'll look around a year from now and think, "Wow, I created this amazing life."

Your Unique Magic

One of the best part about working with your guides on your soul path is that you can more easily access how you're meant to help others in the world. Because no matter what your soul is asking you to do, the work always includes helping others in some way. Even if it seems like a solitary pursuit, such as writing or creating a piece of art or even filling out a spreadsheet, we do this work so that others will be able to take something from it and in some way improve their own lives.

You can start by asking your guide: "What is my magic or medicine?" If those words don't resonate for you, you could phrase it more like, "What unique gifts do I bring to the world?" These are some of the most important and powerful questions that I've worked on with my own guides.

And if you still feel like you absolutely have to have a name for the work that you want to offer right now, let's pick a name and run with it. Whatever you decide on right now can be changed later if you decide it doesn't work for you. If you're opening up your own business, you can change your website, your business cards, and even your business name. If you're following a different path in your career, you can always change jobs again. And if you're attempting a new creative endeavor like writing that book; or taking up painting, pottery, or book-binding, you can always, always, always create something new.

What's important about naming things is focusing on what feels the most true for you right now, regardless of what the world calls the work you do. We're looking for *your* right words, not anyone else's. Our work is always about tuning in and discovering what is right and true for us, even when it doesn't look or sound "normal."

Let's discover what you would most like to call yourself or the work right now, and keep going. Your guides may have some clear guidance for you... or they might not. I don't always get super clear guidance around titles for my books or programs or services, but eventually the name will come to me, and I don't feel the need to question whether the name came from my helping spirits or the logical and rational part of my mind. And really, why do we make those distinctions, anyway? It's all Source energy.

JOURNEYING WORK

Explore Your Sacred Path with Your Helping Spirits

In the following exercise, you'll be invited to explore additional aspects along your sacred path. Choose one to two prompts that feel most resonant and interesting for you to explore with your helping spirits in order to gain additional levels of clarity and certainty around your sacred path.

- If I were living in total integrity with myself, what would I be doing?
- If I could find more authenticity in my life and work, what would that be?
- What are my deepest desires?
- What am I missing in my life?
- If I was living according to my highest purpose, what would that feel like? What would I be doing differently?
- If I knew what my sacred path looked like, I would …
- If I were given full permission to follow my soul, I would …
- If I had complete control over my life, I would …
- What am I being called to do?
- What else is there for me?
- What is my unique magic, medicine, or gifts?

Naming your work:

- How would I most like to call myself?
- What perspectives can I see around the words I choose to use for my title?
- What words feel aligned and exciting to me?
- What words are important to my higher self?

- How can I bring lightness and joy to this naming process?
- What would feel most aligned to call the work that I do?
- Please show me additional elements to my most ideal life.
- Please show me how my family might be affected when I follow my sacred path.
- Please show me part of the beauty and the grace possible when I follow my sacred path.
- Please offer a healing around times when I haven't followed my sacred path in the past.

Chapter 6
Finding Time for Your Journeys

Although journeying work can be done at any time, there's a reason nearly every book on spirituality out there tells you that you've got to start your day with a regular morning practice. (Cue the eye roll, I know!) The reason so many people are banging this drum is because the spiritual discipline and commitment required of you to get up early and meditate or journey does many powerful things for you, other than delaying your coffee or your Facebook feed scroll-time. Not that you were scrolling on Facebook in the morning anyway … right?

What can a morning journey do for you?

- Help you break the old patterns of thoughts that have kept you in the same life patterns you're currently in
- Set aside time for your divine, intuitive side to problem-solve

- Create new pathways and synapses in your brain
- Set up your day for ease, joy, and flow

Also, it feels really freaking good to start your day this way.

You might be asking yourself if you actually have to wake up early. The answer is no, of course not! This is your life. Do whatever you damn well please. And if you already have some sort of reflective practice that you do every day at three o'clock in the afternoon or nine o'clock at night, by all means continue doing it at that time. But if you don't, are new to meditation and journeying practices, or have been inconsistent with your spiritual work, then let me highly encourage you to start a morning routine.

Trick Your Brain with the "Fifteen-Minute" Trick

If you're still not on board with the idea of daily practice, just tell your brain it's only for fifteen minutes—that's all you have to commit to. You might find you enjoy your time so much that you choose to stay and journey or meditate even longer. You might find yourself excited to jump out of bed a little bit earlier every day so that you can get in this very special time with yourself in order to create new levels of peace, calm, and abundance in your life. Or, you might find that after doing this for about a month—nope, you still really hate mornings. And that's okay. It's still your life. You always get to choose.

More Tricks for Journeying in the Mornings

Don't use your phone as an alarm clock. If you need an alarm clock, buy one for $15. And if you ask your body or helping spirits to wake you up at a certain time, you might start to notice that you'll be woken up at that time.

I suggest using a computer, tablet, or device that doesn't have notifications or easy access to social media on which you can access music or drumbeats for your journeying. Otherwise, it's just way too easy to start scrolling through your socials, especially if that's your normal habit. And if you're trying to break the habit of checking Facebook or email first thing in the morning, it's going to take a little bit of willpower. Since we know from research that willpower is limited every day, you're going to want to use your little bit of willpower to get your butt into a chair for a journey.

If you have many responsibilities to others, consider asking family members or partners for help in what you need. It can feel incredibly weird and awkward, especially if you've always given your time and energy to everyone else. However, it's entirely possible to say, "Hey, I need about fifteen minutes to myself every morning. Can you give me that?" It might mean alternating days for dog walking, cat feeding, child minding, and so on.

When you have little-bitty ones, the morning routine will of course be harder. If you're breastfeeding at five a.m., it's probably going to be really hard to wake up at six a.m. for a journey. There isn't one simple solution when you have smaller children. However, it is possible to find a time that works for you. I used to get up earlier than my oldest son to meditate in the mornings before work, and then with my second one, I would nurse first and then have my husband watch the kids for half an hour or so in the mornings.

If you don't manage to get to your journeys in the morning, try to find the earliest opportunity for this work. You may get a pass on the mornings, but hopefully you can still find fifteen minutes in your day for yourself. If you don't, things absolutely have to shift. Get the help you need. Get the support you need. Ask for it. Seek it out. You deserve fifteen minutes to yourself every day. I also recognize that my ability to say "ask for help and get it" is coming from a place of extreme privilege. Not everyone can hire someone to come in and help out, or seek out family members to help out, or get help from a partner or spouse. But often, there is a solution.

One friend of mine had a membership to the YMCA and would plop her kids in the kids' club and then go meditate in the locker room. Quite a few people I know just get up earlier than their kids to do this work. And remember that you can always ask your helping spirits for help in finding a solution too!

Letting Go of Housework to Create More Time

My friend Kay is a stay-at-home mama and was feeling really anxious a lot of the time, even though she was meditating every day. When I listened to what her day consisted of, I could see why: she made three meals a day for her family and then every night after tucking the kids in bed, she spent hours cleaning up the house.

If, like Kay, you're finding yourself saying things like, "But I don't have time," perhaps you could consider letting go of some of the housework. Most of us have internalized the belief that our house has to be perfect—it has to look perfect, and we have to be perfect, etc. Walking the sacred path means letting go of all those expectations and beliefs, such as, "a good mom does these things..." or "a good spouse/partner does these things...."

We worry that people will think we're unclean, a slob, a bad mom, or a bad wife if the house isn't clean. I mean, who decided that the dishes have to get done every day? Who are we really trying to impress here? Our spouses? Our parents? That's some old, old stuff right there.

And if you truly love to clean and it's truly what lights up your soul, continue to do what lights up your soul! But if you're spending over an hour every day on cleaning your house and aren't doing the things you know you want to be doing, something has to change. That means that you'll have to put your dreams and your spiritual path ahead of the dishes. Imagine if you were spending that hour on you and your dreams instead. What could you get done in that hour?

There will always be something that keeps you from following your path, if you allow there to be, like driving the kids to school, the job, the cucumbers that need to be pickled, the doctor's appointments, time spent taking care of aging parents, etc. I'm not making light of these very real responsibilities (except maybe the cucumbers), but you've got to *also* make following your dreams a priority or it won't happen. No one else will make it a priority—not your spouse, your children, or your parents. You have to claim permission to have a different life than the one you have right now and be willing to go after it with your whole heart.

I don't want to be harsh, so please consider this just a loving and compassionate little kick in the bum: Do you want to have the floor mopped every day, or do you want to actually follow your path? And if you're asking just how will it all get done, let me gift you with a little mantra of mine: the dishes always get done. They just do. However, I don't prioritize doing dishes in my life. If the dishes don't get done in the evening, oh well. Sometimes they sit there in soapy water until the next morning, when it's my husband's turn. Sometimes I do them late in the evenings. Other times, I do them in the afternoon. Sometimes I get my kids to do them. And once per week, a very nice person comes in and helps to do the dishes. But they always, always, always get done. Only so many dishes can pile up before someone needs a clean one.

Your priority is to follow your joy, your bliss, and your happiness, which will most likely mean that other things are removed from your priority list. As soon as you decide that you get to claim this time back for yourself, you will absolutely find alternative solutions. You will get spouses and children to participate. You will get help as soon as you start looking for alternatives. Often, time expands and we get to have *both* our time and a clean house!

Your soul chose to incarnate in this very real human world with all of our very real responsibilities. We are asked to be light bringers not in spite of our crazy political times, being caregivers, and having businesses or careers, but precisely because of all that's occurring in our current world. We are asked to be healers in a world that so desperately needs our help. In order to do so, though, we'll have to make different choices. We'll also want to consider that everything that we do in our lives is a choice—including volunteering, cooking, and cleaning.

Chores you might choose to see as choices:

- Checking email
- Checking social media
- Hanging out with friends who no longer feel aligned for you
- Cleaning
- Grocery shopping
- Spending hours consoling/counseling friends

In every instance, it is up to you to actively choose which of these things you will continue to do, and then put up boundaries around what is acceptable for you. If you are getting to the end of your week and asking yourself where all your time went, you might want to look at that list of chores and see what could simply be let go of or rearranged. For example, take your kids with you to the grocery store instead of using your precious alone time for that.

Pick Specific Times for Your Sacred Path Work

Committing to specific times for your own personal development or sacred work is really powerful. What if you took every Tuesday and Thursday evening, just for you? Or every Saturday morning? I've taken Saturday mornings as my own ever since my second child was born eight years ago, and now I rarely miss one of these Saturday mornings. That is my time to write, reflect, and enjoy a cup of tea with my writer friends at Starbucks. I push all of my chores to the afternoon, when I'm at my lowest in terms of energy and brainpower, keeping my "golden" mornings to myself or using it for work with clients.

You might also need to leave the house to create space for your sacred path. Find a coffee shop or other space to create space for your sacred path. Just go, and leave the stuff behind. I often leave a messy kitchen behind and head to the coffee shop to do my deep thinking and writing and even, occasionally, client meetings.

JOURNEYING WORK

Find Time for Your Journeys and Your Path

The following questions can be asked of your helping spirits to allow for different ways to view your responsibilities and to find more time for yourself and your sacred path. Reconnect to your guide who has been helping you with your sacred path work and choose a few of the questions that resonate most with you:

- What things could I let go of in my life?
- What situations, processes, friends, and meetings no longer serve me?

- Where have I allowed my energy to be taken by others?
- On an ideal day, how would I like my life to look? When would I take time for emails, phone calls, etc.? Where could I stack up your similar type events or tasks?
- What would I do with my time if I didn't have to clean the house?
- What would I do if someone else took care of all of the chores?
- What are the feelings that come up when I think of not doing all of the chores?

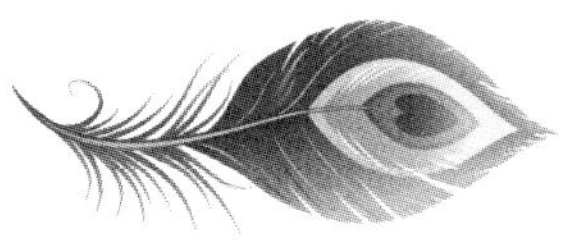

Chapter 7
Releasing Fears of What Others Will Say

When I was a little girl, I dreamed of being a writer. I always had a book in my hands and found my happy place in libraries and schools. I loved words, learning, and stories. When I told my dad my big dream, though, he said, "You know honey, writers don't make a lot of money." He meant to be helpful, but to little Erin, the little eight-year-old girl who dreamed of being a writer, all she heard was, "Give up on that dream. You won't be able to survive as a writer. You'll end up homeless on the streets if you actually follow your dreams." So I shoved that dream down. And even now, as I type these words, I still have to argue with myself. I still have to unravel the belief that there's nothing worthwhile or productive about sitting down to write a book. I mean, I'm not actually making revenue right now.

Certainly, my dad was just doing his best. He wanted to protect me and keep me safe. He wanted to make sure the world didn't hurt me. This isn't about my relationship with my dad—it's about the beliefs so many of us internalized as children. Most likely, you were also given a set of beliefs that said that following your dreams would mean destitution or poverty. Most of us were given a set of beliefs that said there were only certain pathways to becoming "successful," and if we didn't follow those specific paths, then we were being unrealistic, illogical, or impractical.

And now, even as adults, most of us still align our worldview to what we were told by our parents or caregivers. So when we try to follow our dreams, we still worry about what others will think, and if we can be very honest with ourselves, the voices of disapproval that we most feel are those of our primary childhood caregivers or parents. However, it's possible to now release the beliefs that we were given during childhood. We're allowed now to let go of the idea that there is only one way to be "successful" or "productive." We can let go of our ideas of what other people, including parents, might think about our new path.

When Partners or Spouses Aren't Supportive

Some of my friends have spouses who go on the retreats and buy all the crystals and smoke all the herbs. My husband is not one of those. He doesn't understand my spiritual work or what it means. He has a rational, left-brain job in which he is constantly analyzing risk and reward. Overall, he appreciates that following my sacred path makes me happy and that when I take the time for my own pursuits, I'm able to be a better mother and wife and person. However, it took a good minute for us to get to this point.

It's not our job to convince anyone of anything. Other people don't have to believe in our path or "get it." They don't need to change before you can follow your path. Navigating relationships as you explore your sacred path isn't easy, and I don't know anyone for whom the blending of family and spiritual work is easy. What you might find is that as you show up in new and different ways, your family members start to believe in some of the same things you do. They come to realize that there is more to this earth than what we can see with our rational and logical minds. They start to experience some of the strange and mystical magic too. Not because we've convinced them of anything, but because we're embodying the practices and teachings we're being given.

Releasing Fears About What Everyone Else Thinks

My friend Sally is a realtor. And also a psychic. She intuits things about the houses she shows to clients, and she'll often tell her clients to go in a different direction about the house they're showing if she gets a bad reading.

She'd denied this gift for a long time. She'd told herself that it was too weird. She didn't tell many people she had this ability to sense and intuit things that others couldn't.

But then came the billboard.

Sally had been offering readings at a local metaphysical bookstore and unbeknownst to her, they'd put a giant billboard, featuring a picture of Sally and the words, "Psychic Readings!" Um, yeah. Hello, universe. Talk about a spiritual sign!

Maybe you're reading this and thinking, "Well, see, that's a perfect reason to keep quiet about my gifts. I definitely don't want a billboard!" But that was literally a sign from the universe. And now, her clients actually ask her to use her gifts. They want even more of the psychic realtor!

When you try to deny your true gifts, when you try to tuck away the parts of you that are "weird" or "woo-woo" or "out there," then the universe has a way of speaking softly at first, with a gentle whisper to tell you that you're on the right path, anyway. If you don't get that message, then the universe sends ever-louder messages, until finally, there's a shout. "Can you hear me? Yes, you down there! It's time for you to claim your magic!"

All people have intuitive gifts—some of us are just more aware of them than others. It can also feel really, really scary to talk about your gifts with Muggles. So please know there is no rule that says you *must* talk about your work with people who don't appreciate it. In fact, especially in the beginning, it's probably better to protect your work from the eyes of the non-believers. Sometimes, cough, often, these are members of our own family.

Most of us usually have to go through a transition period of slowly showing our "woo woo" panties to those around us. Unfortunately, there is no easy way to do this, other than to walk through that fire. Yep, you will definitely have people who say things to you like, "Do you really do _________?" Fill in the blank with your esoteric practice.

Your fears will probably come up during this process, and you'll be saying to yourself, "But what if they think I'm too weird? Too out there? Can I really do this?" Your friends and family won't necessarily understand or support you as you follow your dreams. And once again, that's okay. You're not doing this for them. You're doing this for you. You're doing this because your soul calls out to you to step onto this path. You're doing this because you can't not do this work. With so much kindness, know that they won't always be supportive. Especially if they aren't following their own path, it will seem scary to them that you're following yours!

You'll have to continually tune into the messages of Source guidance that you are receiving, and know that these are exactly the right messages that will point you forward on your path. Don't seek assurances and guarantees from the people around you, or even from what anyone else has done before you. Because there's never a point where the future or even the current moment is known to us. How could we ever know what the universe has in store for us? The universe doesn't even know. We are continually operating in the most beautiful unknown; that's what makes this existence so beautiful. If this life were all mapped out, you'd quickly tire of this existence.

You're continually being given the opportunity to reconnect in with your divine essence and call on that divinity in order to co-create what you'd like to see in your world, and at the same time, holding on to the knowing that nothing happens as one plans it to happen. And this is good. We're continually realigning, staying in a state of constant growth and change. Imagine a pool of stagnant water: mold has an easy chance to take hold. Instead, you're living in the midst of a rushing, clear stream. Which can be both scary and exhilarating, but you wished for this, your soul wished for this. What other reason is there to be embodied on this earth than to experience the thrills of moving along this swiftly flowing river called life?

This is the path of your highest good. Continually seek it out. Continually come back to this place of magic, where you are loved and tended to by the awesome power of Source energy. Ask for that energy to follow you throughout your day, to create a beautiful place of light and love all around you.

The mission is not to have it all figured out, because there will never, ever, be a moment in time when you have it all figured out. When you do have those moments where you feel like you've finally nailed it all down, then you can be pretty assured that change is coming. One of the laws of the universe is change, all the time: nothing is at rest. Even the rocks are changing around you.

Don't ask for everything to remain as it is. You wouldn't even desire that outcome. Instead ask: how can I find myself more joyously in the stream of life? How can I allow myself to steer my raft, to chart my course, on this beautiful river of all that is good?

You get to create what you desire in conjunction with the most powerful of all forces: consciousness. You get to choose, right now, a different reality than the one that you see around you. But it doesn't start with a huge swift jump. It starts with a gentle, gentle tug. No need for the grand gesture. Instead, explore a little of what you desire, right now. Create a little bit of that, right now.

JOURNEYING WORK
Release Beliefs around What Others Think

Connect to your sacred path helping spirit to explore and release beliefs. Once you feel that deeper connection, you might choose to ask some of the questions in the following list. Exploring the beliefs that others have passed on to you and then lovingly releasing and healing them is perhaps some of the most important work in this book.

- Where can I allow in more of the light of change in my life?
- What am I being shown to step into more today?
- How can I surround myself with positive energy in the face of obstacles, even in the form of other people's opinions?
- Where can I let go of judgment from others?
- Where can I let go of judgment I've placed on others?
- How do I walk this path while being in deeper connection with my partner?
- How do I form a connection that is deeper than our current relationship?
- How do I see their worthiness in my relationship?
- How do I claim my power in this relationship while still honoring theirs?
- Please show me beliefs I have held on to from others.
- Please show me beliefs I have carried with me in my ancestral lineage.
- What messages have I received about success?

- What would I be doing if I didn't have to be "successful"?
- What was my mother's version of success? What was my father's? My family's? My culture's?
- How can I help to heal these beliefs?

Chapter 8
TAKING ACTION

When doing spiritual work, what can sometimes happen is that we use it as an escape mechanism, a way to avoid moving forward, saying things like, "My helping spirits haven't shown me the path yet."

While this work is really cool, you still have to take action in the real world. You can't simply rely on your helping spirits to send everything to you. If you were driving your car to get to a destination, at some point, you'd actually have to get in the car and hit the gas pedal—you couldn't get there by continually hitting the brakes.

If you want things to change in your life, journeying alone won't change them. You'll have to take this work and do something with it. You still have to write the book. You still have to create the business. You still have to get your business cards made, find the new job, or plan the trip.

There's usually something you're being asked or called to do, but just know that *there's no one right step* along this path. The only right steps are the ones that appear before you. You're going to have to step forward into the chasm without knowing whether the steps will appear beneath your feet. You're absolutely stepping into the unknown, where there are no guarantees of anything. And with each step, you'll continually be supported by your guides, those who follow the light, and your inner being. Follow her. She knows the way. Simply ask, "What would excite my inner being to be doing today? What would light her up, make her so excited to be going today? Where would I find the most joy in my workings with others? What would excite me to create, to grow into, to find for myself?"

Know that all these steps are helping to create the brighter world that you would like to see; your journey will become a shining beacon for others, both within your own family and without, to see that it is possible to follow the bright light of your heart and create the world you want to see around you.

When you seek only to be connected with the light and follow the nudges of your higher self, you are never lost. You are found, within the love that surrounds you at all times. Seek today only to be gifted the clarity that comes from taking one step. And know that if you are having trouble with getting started, then the problem is fear. We'll be diving deep into the work that will help with all sorts of fears over the next few chapters.

Creating the Confidence to Take Action

Dan is a successful commercial real estate broker. During our sessions together, Dan and I worked on growing his businesses by connecting to his helping spirits. He shared with me recently about the two owls nesting near his home. "I hear them calling to each other from time to time. Occasionally I am blessed to see one of them perched in different trees on the property. I journeyed to learn what they mean to me. I went to a place high on top of a mountain. Owl came and told me to listen carefully for words not spoken and to see things that others do not see."

Dan realized this message was about his real estate work, and he felt validated about the things he was doing with his clients to find properties. He knew that the "deft flying that owls do means that I can navigate where no one else goes."

In order to walk your own sacred path, you're going to be asked to cultivate your inner power. It's not necessarily the same thing as confidence, but the two share many traits. And luckily, your helping spirits can help you to create that sense of inner power.

This version of power is not the masculine version, the one in which our need to be "right" is more important than living in harmony with the world around us and has led to the suffering of millions through war, conflict, and displacement. Instead, this is a version of inner power in which we no longer need to defend our ways of being but instead can simply be in harmony. From our example, others might see that a different path is possible for them too.

How do we actually create confidence? You're not going to like this answer: through taking aligned actions. When we're reaching for something larger than what we currently have but don't believe that it's possible for us, our subconscious mind will find many ways to block ourselves from having what we want. The good news is that we can combat this by taking aligned actions, by doing those things that speak to our heart.

When we talk about cultivating confidence for our path, the question we must then ask is: where am I being called to step forward? In order to create confidence, you must step forward and take those steps, even without feeling confident enough already, trustting that the steps you're being shown are exactly the right steps. After all, there's no secret manual for creating something no one else has ever created before. Even if someone has done something similar to what you want to do, their path won't be just like yours because there is no other you in the entire universe, and there might not ever be a time where you feel confident enough. Instead, simply step forward, even when you're scared. And remember that you have help in the form of your helping spirits to guide you.

Now is your opportunity to invite in the healing power of Source as you create your new endeavors. What will you choose on these inspired pathways? What will you choose to give voice to? These are questions that you must ask with the highest integrity, and then follow that guidance without fear.

Know that anything is possible. You come from the same stuff that made the planets; you are the same substance as the infinite universe, and need not hew to any known structures or outlines. Instead, follow your internal guidance when creating new creations and allow the wisdom of your highest self to shine forth.

Releasing the Fear of Failure

At the end of last year, I was feeling kind of lost and stuck in my business, and I was attracted to a group coaching program in which we would learn to run our own successful group coaching programs. I had run group coaching programs in the past but hadn't charged a lot of money for them. I thought that perhaps this new coach would give me the answers I was seeking. Fewer clients, but more money? Sign me up!

I thought I needed to copy that other coach's ways of marketing and pricing. Well, that experiment ended in disaster: only three people signed up for my group, and I'm used to having group programs where at least six to nine people sign up. I had let myself be pulled out of what was right and true for me. Although I knew how I normally liked to market and even price my groups, I had let myself believe that someone else knew better and that I might "fail" if I tried to do it my own way. It wasn't until I tuned in to the ways I most liked to share and market my group programs that I was able to successfully fill another program.

When you're trying to avoid failure, you might also seek outside answers and reassurances, which is normal. Most of us were taught as children that other people had the right answers, so we sought reassurance and confirmation from our teachers, parents, and friends. Indeed, your very nervous system is programmed to avoid being wrong and thereby potentially lose your family's love and care. As you try to do something different in life, your nervous system and subconscious mind will definitely tell you to play it safe; do the "right" thing and avoid failure. But what if, instead, you could really be with that feeling in your body and energetic system? What if you noticed what came up for you and spoke gently with that feeling of failure? Work with your guides to see where this feeling comes from and then release it.

We've all been told that the answers exist somewhere outside of ourselves, that someone out there holds the secret to the "right way" to find clients, make money, or be successful, or take the first damn step on the path, but no one else can ever have your unique answers. You can release the fears of failure with your guides and then create the powerful feelings you want to be true in your body. Watch how an entirely new reality emerges, one where the fear of failure no longer holds you back.

In actuality, there is no such thing as failure. Everything is just data; if what you're trying to do doesn't work the first time, perhaps there's another way to go about it or another way to tweak or improve whatever you're trying to accomplish.

And if you've worked through some of those specific fears and are now seeking an actual plan or more definitive answers to the question of how, the best advice I've ever heard is to just start—build the airplane as you're flying it. Just take one step.

When I started life coaching school, our teachers asked us to start coaching the other students the very first weekend. I was nervous! What did I know about coaching? I hadn't learned anything yet. But after a few months of school, I realized something very profound: there was not going to be some magical thing that occurred at the end of my schooling that would confer upon me the ability or the right to start coaching. I would still have to put myself out there and get clients somehow. Having a certificate hanging on my wall wasn't going to change the fact that I would still need to find clients.

So, I started taking clients even before we were done with school. I don't really know how it even happened, so I can't tell you how I got my first client except that I simply announced to the universe that I was a coach. I announced it to my friends and family, offering extremely affordable sessions, something like fifty dollars per hour. That probably helped. By the time we finished life coaching school, I was already coaching. I did the same thing with all my other modalities. As soon as I learned a practice, I would begin to offer it to my clients.

If you're asking how to make money from this, or how to get started right now, here's the answer: you just start. As soon as you take your first dollar for what you want to do, then you know it's possible to actually make money from it. As soon as you put out your first offer, your first anything, then you're doing the thing!

Okay, I know that's not what you wanted to hear. You want to hear all the actual steps, the strategies, the exact outline to following your dreams. Really, though, you just start. Put out an offer. Any offer. Share with people about what you're offering: readings, healings, coaching sessions, mentoring sessions, personal soul guidance sessions—whatever your soul is showing you, simply let people know about it in some way.

There's no secret path to starting a business, changing your career, or making money doing what you want to do. Simply decide you're going to go out there and do your soul work and then do it. Keep doing it, even when the chips are down, the dog throws up on the rug, and the babysitter cancels on you.

My client J. really struggled with getting started. She had amazing plans for what she wanted to offer in her non-profit, but she was spending a lot of time on the organizational aspects of her business, including the legal set-up and finding an accountant and bookkeeper.

So let me gently offer this: you don't need an accountant or a bookkeeper until you're earning money in your business. When you start earning more than a few hundred dollars a month, then maybe it's time to hire both of those. Earn a single dollar for your business, *then* worry about the rest. Obviously, I'm not an attorney or an accountant, so don't take my advice on the legal aspects of starting a business. But if you live in the United States, you can usually take twenty minutes to create an LLC online with your state, and boom—you're a business.

If you're reading this and thinking, "But I need to wait until I finish that program or get the certification first," or "I need a website first," then let me say this with so much kindness: that's just fear talking. You don't need most things people think are needed to get started. You can already offer something to the world, right now. Later, when you do finish that program or get that certification, or when you establish your legal entity, or finish your website, you'll be one step further on the path, but none of those things are absolutely required in order to start doing the thing you want to do.

If what you want to do requires certification prior to opening a practice (e.g., massage, chiropractic), by all means, wait until you have the piece of paper. Let's not do anything illegal here. Most of the time, however, we don't need a piece of paper to get started. Coaches, guides, and mentors of all kinds don't usually require certification.

Releasing Worry Over the Past or Future

Another common impediment to starting is worrying about something that happened in the past or something that might happen in the future. In these instances, there's no use worrying. Worry has never done anyone any good. I believe humans used to exist in a more peaceful brain state, in which we only needed our worried, beta brain waves for dangerous situations. But since the advent of clocks and measurements and metrics, our brains were asked to live more outside the present moment, turning most of us into the worried people we are today. While we can't measure the brain waves of Paleolithic people, the take-away here is that the more you can work with your guides to release worries around what has already happened or what might happen in the future, the closer to happiness you might come.

You might now be thinking, "But isn't worrying necessary? Without worry, wouldn't we all just walk out in front of cars?" I've asked myself the same thing. Letting go of worry doesn't mean letting go of common sense, though. You don't worry that you're going to burn your hand on the stove when it's on, *and* you would still not touch the burner. Worrying does nothing good for us or even on behalf of others. After all, has worrying ever changed anything for the better? Instead, the worry just creates more stress, which we all know is harmful to our health. And the good news is that you can work with your guides to both release worry and to find answers to whatever you're most worried about.

JOURNEYING WORK
Clarity and Confidence

Connect to the helping spirit of your sacred path to ask questions that will create more confidence and clarity.

- What most needs to happen, right now, today?
- Where am I being called to lead and show up more in my life?

- How could I best create a plan for following my path?
- What real world things must I consider for following my path?
- What can I know right now about the words for my work in this world?
- What can you show me about where this fear of failure comes from?
- What is this fear trying to show me?
- Dear guides, what can you show me about my past childhood experiences that made me fear failure?
- Please help me to lovingly release this feeling of failure. (This is healing work to be done by your helping spirits—not by you!)
- How can I lovingly release the memories associated with this fear of failure?
- What can I be shown about my steps forward?
- What sort of posture or perspective would I like to hold instead?

Chapter 9
Releasing Overwhelm

My client Lisa wanted to move somewhere with her family that was more in line with her values and the way she wanted to raise her children, but she felt as though a big block was in her way. She said, "I've tried everything, but it just feels like I can't get past it. Our family is still in the same place we were a few months ago."

Whether we use the words "stuck," "lost," or "blocked" or "overwhelmed," I believe these are times when we can tune in to the wisdom of our helping spirits and receive detailed guidance. The key here is that we must follow through on that guidance, no matter how silly it sounds.

When I guided Lisa in a journey, she worked with Bear, her helping spirit, and was shown that an energetic release needed to happen. Bear lovingly did the work on her behalf. The next week, Lisa emailed me to say her husband had been offered a job interview in Denver. The block was gone!

You can connect to your guides and allies whenever you're feeling stuck or lost and ask for support and advice. Even when the advice we've been given feels too weird, too out there, or too simple, this is most likely exactly the guidance that we need to follow.

We get tripped up when the advice from our guides to move through stuck or lost times is to simply rest or just "be." It's important to remember that the stuck phases, the lost phases, the "not fully plugged in" phases are absolutely necessary parts of the generative cycles of creativity. These are the fallow times, when the seeds that have been planted are being nurtured within the dark loam. Your seeds need this time. You need this time.

When you move through the stuck-ness, what emerges will be so powerful, so beautiful, and so rewarding, that you'll wonder if you were ever even stuck at all.

How to Work with Stuck Energies or Blocks

Okay, yes, I know, I hear you. You want the real stuff. You want the "yeah, but how do I get rid of this freaking block?" Firstly (and I'm only sort of kidding), stop calling it a block. Think about what would happen if we gave ourselves so much grace to know that these are normal cycles in our lives? It doesn't mean that if you're feeling stuck that you try to push through without acknowledging that there's a block at all. Indeed, sometimes the block is just fear. But other times, it's a resetting phase, a fallow time, a time for you to gather your energies for the emerging spring.

One way to discern the difference between a fallow period and fear is to have a conversation with your guides. You might also do some journaling, tapping, or other somatic work around the block.

We all have days and moments where we feel overwhelmed, confused, and at a loss as to how to go forward. These are the times when we most need the help of our helping spirits and our sacred power. One thing that always helps me is to get outside and connect to the earth. When in doubt, head out! I'll head outside and lie down on my front lawn, making sure to sink my feet into the grass. It might be harder to do if you live in a more urban area, but the reward of finding a park or small patch of grass where you can lie down and look up at the trees is *so* worth it.

When we forget about our connection to the Earth, we can stumble, lose our way, and get trapped in cycles of fear, disappointment, overwhelm, and procrastination, all of which cause us to shut down and not do the work we need to do. All it takes is a few moments of being outside again and connecting to the earth for us to feel into what might be most aligned to do next. What most needs to happen for us to feel truly aligned?

The feeling of being overwhelmed usually begins when we listen to outside messages about what we need to be doing, but remember that we *always* have a choice in our actions. You can choose not to take that client call. You can choose to walk away from that social media post. You can choose to let someone else pick up the kids from school.

So often, when we sit with our heart space, we discover that the things we thought "needed" to be done actually don't. We can always ask for an easier pathway from our guides. The answer we receive might be simply to rest, but sometimes even asking the question helps me find a much easier pathway to my end goal. For instance, I was stressing out one evening because I still needed to make dinner for two hungry kids and prep for a class I taught regularly. I also still needed to go to the local office store to make better color copies and couldn't see how that could all get accomplished in a timely way, especially during Atlanta's epic rush hour traffic. So I went outside, rested in the grass, and asked how I could make this easier. The answer came to me that I already had color copies from a previous workshop. (Yeah, this should have been obvious, but it wasn't at the time.) The answer from my guides saved me that big trip to Kinko's and allowed me to show up fully for my workshop, with children happily fed.

Whenever you're feeling overwhelmed, simply stop what you're doing. Get outside. Sink your feet into the earth. Take off your shoes, feel the ground beneath your feet, even if just for a moment. Feel the elements, even if it's raining or cold. Relax into the loving embrace of the

Earth Mother. Allow her to support your steps and create guidance in your life. Let go of the need to be busy by tuning into the natural rhythms of your body and the earth's cycles.

You might question how you can possibly get things done in the "real world" if you're spending all of this time underneath the trees. But the "real world" is only something you've created with your thoughts, and you can uncreate it too. Every time you listen to the calling of your heart and soul instead of the outside messages of striving and doing, you'll feel a lightness and sense of purpose, and even if there are things that truly "have to get done," you'll be able to do them with a much lighter heart. Discover the bliss that can come from tuning in to what it is that really needs to be done, and what can wait. Lean into the happiness that can result in understanding your unique rhythms and the divine timing of it all. Feel the creative movement that can happen when you are tuned in to the channel of pure beingness.

You're a being of infinite light, so why constrain yourself to the dim glow of the computer or the flash of the television screen? Can you instead ask "What would most serve the world right now? What would most serve me right now? What would make my heart sing with joy?"

You might think, "but I have all of these responsibilities and these clients and these tasks to do today." Ask yourself where you can let go even more, where you can move into the energy of guided flow even more. You have answers within already, but sometimes it's hard to see those answers, because that would mean that you would need to question the very fabric of your life.

We humans have somehow created a false world in which we believe that it is only through "doing enough" that we can ever possibly be enough, and though you may already know that this isn't true, perhaps like me, you still struggle with questions like: Who will you be if you're not doing? Who will you be if you're not constantly creating? Who will you be if you're no longer identified with your job, title, or career?

If you start to ask those questions, a great darkness or a time of change might arise. However, you have the ability to tune into the power of Source with your helping spirits and receive support as you move through these questions.

JOURNEYING WORK

Release Being Stuck or Overwhelmed

Ask to connect with your body protector. Once connected, ask your body protector to guide you to a place of power where you can be in dialogue with the block or stuck or overwhelmed energy itself.

Consider the following questions:

- What do you represent?
- What is beyond this energy?
- What am I being shown here?
- What is mine to own, and what belongs to others here?
- Is there a healing that needs to be offered?
- What would feel aligned to release from my life right now?
- Where can I allow more ease and flow and lightness?
- What boundaries might I create in order to allow ease and flow?

Part 3

Abundance

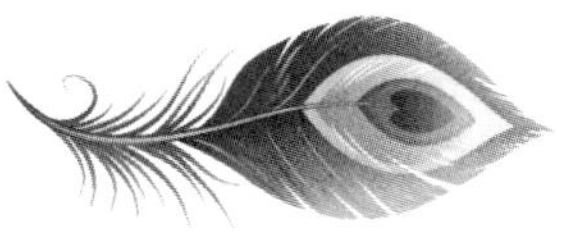

Chapter 10 WORKING WITH YOUR ABUNDANCE GUIDES

Our abundance guides are here to help us to be in a state of thankfulness and love as much as possible, which is the path to abundance. Working with your guides will help you step into your best and highest self at all moments and a space of inner power and deservingness, which is such a perfect state to manifest your dreams.

We're asked to continually step into the state of love, wherein we tune in and attempt to understand and love the person across from us, no matter who they are—a spouse, child, family member, or someone of the opposing political party. Even if they've recently triggered us, or said or done something we don't like, we're being asked to truly transmute our own negativity into something beautiful.

The spinning of dross into gold is done through shifting emotions from anger, frustration, and annoyance into forgiveness. When you're angered, frustrated, or even mildly annoyed, you're blocking the flow of your inner power and the Divine, obstructing the signals and signposts that point you in the way of opportunities. In other words, you're blocking money from flowing to you! Luckily, your guides are great at helping you unblock anything standing in your way to allow for more abundance.

Your guides can also help with more practical questions around money and financial security, e.g., "Will this be financially rewarding to me or not?" One note of caution when asking questions around money or financial success: as with everything, our guides don't see the world in terms of black or white or good or bad. When we ask for their help, we must understand their versions of success and happiness might be different from ours. When we ask questions such as, "Should I take this job?" what we usually mean is something like, "Is this job going to help me to be financially stable? Is this job going to make me happy?" Your helping spirits are seeing your path from the perspective of many lifetimes and of your soul. To continue the example, they might see how this particular job will teach you to no longer bow to others' authority—but maybe that's not something your human body really wants to learn right now. As always when doing this work, ask open-ended questions. If you're asking for help with more money or clients, ask open-ended questions about what it would mean to have more of those in your life, as opposed to questions such as, "Can you show me how I can get more money?"

My first journey to my own abundance guide brought me deep within the belly of the great pyramids to a deep and ancient river beneath the pyramids, where I met Horus, the falcon-headed god of the ancient Egyptians. I was freaked out. He's scary and super powerful, and all I could think was, "I don't even know enough about Egyptian gods. How can this be happening?" As always, I needed to let go of my rational mind in order to deepen into the work. Once I did, the god showed me a process for connecting with him in a way that honors his powerful energy as well as protects me from being drawn into his energy too much. Now when I'm struggling with money decisions in my business, including topics such as how to raise my prices, I can journey to Horus and ask those questions.

In another example of working with abundance guides, in a recent abundance retreat I hosted, a powerful healer named Debbie shared her experience of connecting to her abundance guide, a star being draped in magnificent green and gold jewels. She asked a star being who doesn't care about money why they'd be her abundance guide. The guide answered, "Because I know how incredibly powerful you are. You should be that powerful around money; you should be magnificently abundant." Debbie has since gone on to get herself an ever bigger income in her healing business, and she has even been featured as a healer with a prominent group online.

Working with a Guide for Your Business or Career

In addition to your abundance guide, you might also enjoy connecting with a guide specifically for your business or career. When Debbie did this in our retreat, she shared how she was led into a clearing in a gentle forest surrounded by a circle of stones where she met her guide: an incredible jaguar. He had a collar with three things that resembled feathers or darts.

When she asked Jaguar what she needed to do as related to her magic, Jaguar answered: to embody it. She was shown an image of herself in her healing room and how she might pull things from all the techniques she'd learned. He gave her the message that she would be a better healer if she just embodied her healing modalities. "I saw myself standing in the middle of the circle of stones. My clothes and body were simply shimmering golden light. My arms were raised, my magic fully embodied," Debbie shared.

Words don't convey how powerful connecting to a guide can be. And because this work is happening in the slightly altered state where your conscious mind is no longer in charge, the words and images your guides share with you are imprinted upon your subconscious, meaning you get a real upgrade to the old patterns and conditions that might have been running you in the past, allowing you to access even more abundance.

With your business or career guide, you might ask about specific directions you wish to go in, or insight into someone else's perspective so that you are better able to reconcile or connect with this person in your business or career. You could also work together to let go of any fear that arises as you go after something specific. Ultimately, working with your guides in your business or career is about seeing how you can show up more with love.

If you already have a business of your own, I'm sure you've had the experience before of getting angry at mythical clients who aren't showing up, saying to yourself, "But where are they? Why don't they see how cool this work is? Didn't they see my amazing post/offer/launch?" Obviously, that's not a state of mind or energetic attraction that's going to attract new clients. Just like the needy person at the bar is avoided, potential clients will avoid you if they sense that you're needy, desperate, or frustrated. Letting go of that neediness with your guides is a powerful pathway to opening up to more abundance.

JOURNEYING WORK

Connect with an Abundance Guide

Connect with an abundance guide. You might ask the following or similar:

- Please show me what it would mean to truly expand into abundance today.
- Please show me how we can best work together.
- Please show me more about my path to abundance.
- How can I invite in more abundance into my life?
- What would feel fulfilling around my purpose and money?
- What can I know now about my path to abundance?
- May I receive a healing around abundance?

With your guide for your career or business you might ask:

- How do I let go of fears that arise as I pursue what I love?
- What can you show me about a particular person or situation?
- How can I bring a deeper level of understanding to this particular situation?
- What can I see or know about my business or career path?

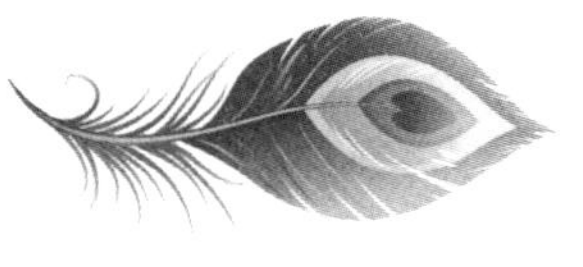

Chapter 11
CREATING THE VISION

One of the most powerful tools to shift your reality and create abundance in your life is your imagination. Usually, imagination is dismissed in our culture as something that belongs to children's fantasies, fairytales, and daydreams. However, as more research emerges about the mind, more results are uncovered that show that our thoughts absolutely have enormous power over our outer reality. We see this in the healthcare field, where (controlling for other factors) depressed patients have worse health outcomes and optimistic patients have better ones. The power of thought extends much further than health, of course; we all have the power to shift anything in life by simply imagining a new reality.

Imagination and strong emotion together form the basis for manifesting your ideal world and the abundance you desire. And while the word "manifesting" often gets a bad rap, we're actually manifesting all the time, though we don't necessarily call it that. Oftentimes, we're worrying about something or picturing an outcome that we don't want. Instead, you could use that awesome power of your mind to spend time imagining what you desired, instead. The great news with consistently utilizing your imagination to manifest your desires is that even if what you're imagining doesn't come to pass, you'll still come out feeling better than if you'd spent the time worrying about it.

Also, a time lag exists on this physical plane between our thoughts and what comes to pass in constructed reality. You might not think of this time lag as something beneficial, but just imagine if every thought that came into your head immediately became real. All those thoughts like "what if this ladder fell on my head?" or even more negative thoughts might also manifest instantly. In actuality, it's a good thing that we have a time lag for our thoughts to become real. This way, you have time to define your desires and focus on bringing forth only what you want to have. The key here is to consistently keep imagining what you wish to see happen in your world with emotion and joy.

Often when people start working with the power of imagination and creating the vision, they'll feel like it's not working for them. Shifting your entire thought process is hard. One of the best things that you can do is to notice and bring attention to the thoughts you don't like and then instead imagine what you do desire, over and over. Continue to imagine the outcomes you wish to have, even for small things. Set your intention before entering a meeting or a conversation with a spouse to have an outcome with the highest good for all and see what happens. Like everything, this work takes practice, and shifting a lifetime of conditioning and programming is harder than simply reading this paragraph; but everything starts with noticing the thought that's arising, and then choosing a different thought and imagining what you do wish to see.

Although it can sometimes feel selfish to give so much attention and focus to the vision of what you want, consider that the universe is expanding through you. As you continually seek out more in your world, Source energy is also expanding through you.

We're all part of a co-creative universe, and the energy of Source is always about expansion and growth, which means that you, too, get to be part of that expansion. When you're fully dialed into desires that truly light up your heart and bring you joy, those are exactly the desires that the universe and Source energy are asking to be expressed through you.

You can easily determine whether the desire comes from ego or Source by tuning in to how the desire feels in your body. Desires that come from Source feel like a beautiful warm hug, like something that feels slightly impossible but also exciting and fun and joyful. The desires from ego are usually more like goals, status symbols, someone else's version of success, things that you *think* you should want at a certain level of income, or things you associate with success or money. None of those things are wrong to desire, of course, and they can certainly be part of your amazing life. However, if you co-create with the power of Source energy by using your imagination instead of trying to force your way to some arbitrary goal or success marker, you'll find the process to be much easier, lighter, and faster.

Bringing Your Desires into Reality

First, see the desired outcome in your mind. Then feel into how good it might feel to have that thing or experience or level of health or level of abundance in your life. Really see yourself having that experience. If it's a new house, see the first time you step through the door. Smell the way it might smell. Hear the sound of the birds outside or your spouse sharing how excited they are to be in the new home. Make it feel real to you.

Everything starts with the vision. If you don't have a clear vision of what you desire, other people's desires will instead become your life, or the default programs that have been running in your life will take over and you'll continue to create the same results and life that you've been experiencing up until now. But if you desire something different in your life, you'll have to create that with the powerful act of visioning and imagining what you do want.

Most often, I don't do visioning work with my spirit guides. I usually sit in a meditative state and then see my future self and check in with what feels exciting and fun. This is where some of my most vivid visions have been created, and those usually come to pass. Right now I'm holding a vision of giving a TED Talk—perhaps by the time you read this book, that will have come to pass!

It might help to work with your guides on seeing the vision more clearly. Often, we don't feel as though we're allowed to have a new vision for our lives or we don't "see" the vision clearly. I've had clients share that when they try to vision, all they see is a blank space. If that describes your experience, ask your guides to open up your visioning abilities. You might also ask your guides to show you different ways to approach the vision you've seen and help you to create it in your outer reality.

JOURNEYING WORK

Open Up to Expansion

First ask which guide might help you in opening yourself up to the vision process. You may or may not meet with your abundance guide; instead you could meet with an ascended master, goddess, light being, or star being.

Once you have made a connection, consider the following requests for clarity:

- Please open up my third eye even more.
- Please show me a way to allow for more expansion in my visions.
- Please show me whatever is possible to know about the power of imagination.
- Please show me how my imagination has helped create change in my life.
- Please show me different pathways toward my vision.

Chapter 12
Shifting Money Beliefs

Sometimes our subconscious mind creates a story about how it's better for us to stay right where we are. At this income level, we're accepted by the people around us. Feelings of anxiety or unease may arise as soon as we try to step outside of our current income level. Those feelings are the subconscious mind doing its job of keeping us safe and loved. Instead of announcing its subconscious blocks, it creates patterns of self-sabotage such as procrastination or not showing up in the desired way. As a result, a large part of working with your guides on abundance is in recognizing and releasing those beliefs, which is an ongoing process. Don't be discouraged if you feel as though you've already done so much of the work of dismantling your beliefs around abundance, either. There's always another level of abundance, which might mean another round of recognizing and releasing old beliefs.

Shifting Your Upper Limit with Your Guides

Right now, you're at the upper level of your income in terms of what you believe is "allowed" for you. Right now, your mind tells you that you're still nice, still spiritual, and still a good person. But if you were to make much more money (an amount that is different for everyone), you might become a different person. You would become someone who is no longer nice, someone greedy, selfish, not giving to others, who doesn't care about little people. Or at least, that's what our subconscious believes to be true. Gay Hendricks introduced this concept of the Upper Limit Problem in his seminal book, *The Big Leap* (Harper-Collins, 2010).

You can expand your own upper limit by asking: what is the level of income or wealth that makes you a different person? At what income level do you become someone who no longer cares about others, according to your personal worldview? At what income level do you need to give away all of your income in order to right yourself with the world again? There's actually no wrong or right answer here. However, no amount of gifting or tithing will take away a feeling of guilt or shame about money if you've passed your upper limit; you'll continue to make things "even" in your mind until you can subconsciously stabilize your income to the point where you feel comfortable again. That's why it's so important to look into these subconscious blocks and tune in to what your guides can share with you.

Most of us grew up with the belief that making money isn't spiritual at all, because most cultures around the world have some version of the spiritual leader who takes an actual or implied vow of poverty, e.g., a priest, nun, guru, or monk. But we live in a different time in which making money is allowed to be part of our spiritual expansion. You can also work with your guides to see how much the universe and Source energy would love to support you in both claiming your spiritual path as well as your financial expansion. This is the middle path, the one in which you get to be both spiritual and wealthy, if that's what you choose for yourself.

We might also have a belief that making money is somehow evil. *And* we could get into a discussion here about what makes something or someone "evil," but for now let's focus on this: Is it truly evil for you to want to make more money? If we can look at the pursuit of money through the energy of Source, we can see that there's nothing morally wrong with wanting more money, even just for the sake of having it. That said, you probably don't want money just to roll around in it. It's more likely you want to have money to give back to the world in some way.

Usually when we're angry that someone else seems to be unethical or lacking integrity in their pursuit of money, there's something we can look at within ourselves. Where have we pursued the money instead of the goodness? Where have we been so narrowly focused on having something that we push away the good? If we can see that thing in others, then it exists within us too.

I'll often see someone on Facebook bashing someone who's made a lot of money. Often the sentiment is something like, "If they make this much money, they should give most of it away." But what if instead of bashing that person with money, you could model the behavior you wish to see in those people? Even if we might wish a certain rich person would give their wealth to us or to some other deserving party, simply handing people large sums of money rarely works unless the recipients' beliefs are also being worked on. If the recipient doesn't believe they deserve or are worthy of the money, it's much more likely for them to spend or lose most of it. That's why you see so many lottery winners losing their money within five years of winning, even millions upon millions.

If you want to become someone who has millions, you will have to believe that it's safe for you to have millions. For the same reason, it's often tough to make huge leaps in our income levels unless we also work on the belief systems beneath the growth. If you believe that you deserve your business or income level to increase at that speed of growth, you'll be able to achieve it. But if you don't believe it's possible for you, you won't.

Becoming aware of these beliefs for the first time can be really tough, but as soon as we start to make the subconscious conscious, we bring light to the darkness. We often cope with emotions and thoughts that we don't want through suppressing, escaping, or expressing them, though at times, even expression isn't enough to release the trigger from our bodies. For instance, if you've ever gotten angry with your children or your partner and then sworn to yourself that you wouldn't do that again, you know that simply having expressed your anger at them isn't enough for that anger to completely go away, and it's because there's a subconscious belief or thought that's beneath the anger. Our job is to see that old, subconscious pattern and work with our guides to release it. And we can also do this with subconscious beliefs around money.

Because when you create more wealth, you're able to do more awesome things for the people and communities you want to support. Just think about all of the good that you want to do with your money, or perhaps already do with your money. Wouldn't it be great to have even more, to do even more good?

It does no one any good for you to remain in poverty, lack, debt, or not-enough-ness around money. It doesn't help the people around you to see you struggling or going without. It doesn't help the communities or people you care about, or your children or your peers. When you create more wealth, others can see that it's possible for someone just like you, with your background, education, or skin color, to follow your light and perhaps even say, "Yes, this is for me too!"

The idea of increasing your individual wealth in order to help end global poverty is controversial. We are all connected to the infinite supply of the universe. After all, if the universe is always expanding, we humans are also meant to expand along all planes—spiritually, emotionally, and financially. If you recognize the truth in these words, then why not you? Why couldn't that expansion be for you too? Even amid whatever is happening in our world, why couldn't that expansion also be possible for you?

Money is not real; it's just a medium of exchange. In our current world, most governments use fiat currency, which means nothing (such as gold or silver) backs it up. Even gold's value is totally arbitrary; we value it over wood, shells, and stones, for instance, all of which have been used as currency in the past, but only because we have chosen to give those things value. Our own stories and beliefs around money are what have created so many of the problems around money, not money itself.

When we do the work of shifting our money beliefs, more of it gets to flow through and to us, allowing for more expansion in the entire world. We get to use the neutral energy of money to be a true force for good when we give it to the organizations, people, and communities of our choosing. And we can do this work of releasing our blocks and welcoming in more abundance with our guides.

JOURNEYING WORK

Heal Money Beliefs, Patterns, and Blocks

Connect with your abundance guide to heal and release money beliefs. As with all of your journeys, check in with your body protector and gate keeper and then ask to be connected to your abundance guide. You'll find your abundance guide is a great one to journey to when you feel general feelings of lack, and you might also play with the following specific questions and statements:

- Please show me my personal beliefs around making money and being spiritual.
- Please show me how I can grow in kindness and financial expansion.
- What is my current upper limit on financial expansion? How can I work with that upper limit?

- Please release any neediness I hold onto around money.
- Please show me what it might look like to expand financially with a loving heart.
- Could I receive a healing around my relationship to money?
- Could you show me what the energy of money looks like?
- Please show me what's my responsibility to hold for the state of the world.
- Please show me how I can best help the world (or a particular situation).

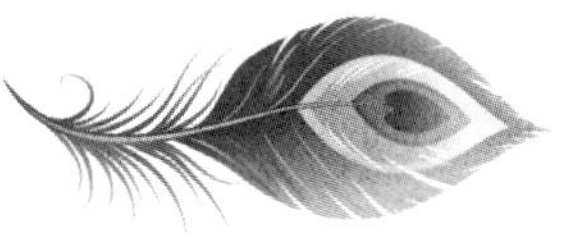

Chapter 13
Becoming Deserving of More

We all have things from our past that we feel guilty about—we've all hurt others or ourselves, and it's common that we feel bad about those experiences and believe they make us somehow unworthy of more. We all have experiences from our past that left us believing: "I did something really wrong, so I don't actually deserve what I currently have, and I definitely don't deserve more." The truth is that you deserve everything you have and whatever you desire for the future, just because you're a human on this planet.

There's no perfect person who's never done anything "wrong" or hurt anyone else. It's not possible to exist on this planet and not hurt someone else. Of course we must be kind, lead with love, and do our inner work of stepping even more into integrity, compassion, and love for others. We must apologize when necessary and work to not do shitty things in the future.

What do our judgments of our worthiness have to do with money? Many of us have a belief that money flows only to those who are "good" or worthy, but money doesn't work this way—if it did, Mother Teresa would have had a palace and former president Trump would be living in a hovel. Money flows to those who believe they deserve it, and there is no absolute set of circumstances in which you will fit someone else's concept of "deserving." Instead, we have to create the belief within that we are deserving, no matter what we might have done in the past or who we might have hurt.

Even though I don't know you, I do know that no matter what you've done, you're still deserving of more. You still deserve to have even more of a beautiful and bountiful life, right now. After all, what would the punishment need to be for what you have done? Haven't you already lived through that punishment? And really, whose idea is punishment, anyway?

Again, being deserving doesn't mean we don't do our work—reparations, apologies, and contrition are all extremely necessary when we've messed up. The good news is that most people are not violent sociopaths with much to apologize for. Most people have the opposite problem: they never feel good enough for the life they've already created, and definitely not for the life they want to create.

I would ask you to consider these questions: When would you be "good enough" for the life you desire? When will you have worked hard enough, done enough good deeds, given enough back, and created enough healing, joy, and love for others in order to be deserving? What if that moment were right now?

Journal your answers to these two questions:

- "Why don't I feel that I deserve to be there?" (With "there" being whatever goal or desire you currently feel is unfulfilled in your life; it might be your income level or a specific achievement, as an example.)
- "Why do I feel that it's easier to be right where I am?"

When you sit with those questions and do some journaling around them, you'll perhaps be able to see the subconscious blocks telling that you don't deserve to be where you want to be. When we're working on attracting money, most often we're actually working on being more deserving. The reason it's easier to manifest a parking space versus a million dollars is that we easily believe we deserve that parking space, but do you believe right now, that you're deserving of a million-dollar business or home? If the answer is no, why not? What do you believe you need to do, have, or be in order to be deserving? How much harder would you have to work? How much healing work would you have to do first? Will there ever be "enough" work or healing that you've done?

Starting to believe that you deserve more money or income just for being human is radical work; most of us were not raised to believe that we were worthy and deserving just for being alive. Let's instead instill a belief that you deserve all good things, right now, just because you're alive on this planet.

Your guides can help you see this different perspective, one in which you are always supported by Source energy in the things you choose to do. Many of us carry a heavy neediness around money, where we keep reaching for it and never finding it. That needy energy is partly why money runs from us—any time we believe we need money, we are believing that it's not already there. In other words, we're more focused on the lack than the having of the thing. If you have an intense need for the money and feel it in your body, you'll most likely receive more lack of the money. Instead, focus on what you do have. Creating gratitude is something your guides are especially amazing at helping with, and your guides can also help you shift any feelings of lack around money. Many of us carry a heavy neediness around money, where we keep reaching for it and never finding it.

Gratitude Stacking

Before we work with your guides on gratitude and deserving-ness, I'll share a few other gratitude hacks so you can instantly feel more deserving. One of my favorite ways for creating gratitude is something called gratitude stacking. Write a list of everything you are grateful for—no need to write things like "sunshine" if that doesn't feel real for you right now. List all the things for which you feel truly grateful right now and include things for which you would like to feel gratitude. For example, the list might look something like:

- This computer, that allows me to communicate with so many people
- My amazing clients
- Mocha lattes
- A brand-new client at my highest-level rate (which doesn't exist yet)
- My new journal, that just looks so beautiful

One caveat is that any additional thing can't feel too huge on the list. For example, if you notice that your mind says, "Oh hell no, we're never going to get a Lamborghini!" you might want to back that down to something that feels more realistic, whether that's a Mercedes or a used Honda. We don't want your subconscious mind to be activated by what you're writing and create an alternative narrative to contend with.

Practice Gratitude Switches throughout Your Day

It's hard to hold on to negative emotions when you're in a state of gratitude. For instance, when I'm driving in traffic and feeling annoyed, I often switch into a positive state by remembering how thankful I am for car insurance. Switching feels really good, especially because I didn't think that car insurance was worth the money in my early twenties and subsequently had some pretty huge car wrecks that I not only paid for out of pocket but almost lost me my driving privileges! I'm now incredibly thankful that I'm able to easily pay for my car insurance.

If you can find just a small sliver of gratitude for whatever you're experiencing, you're already entering the most magical space of power, where everything that occurs happens with and for you—not to you. You can enter this space and find a shift in your perspective in the moment you feel triggered or angry. If you're not able to catch the negative feeling or thought in the moment, do the work with your guides that evening or the next morning to bring a different perspective to your experience so that you can see everything that's happening from the viewpoint of Source and your soul.

Baby-Stepping into Abundance

One practice that will be super helpful to you on the abundance path is to baby-step your way into luxury and abundance. Denise Duffield Thomas shares this idea in her book, *Get Rich, Lucky B*tch* (Hay House, 2018). While the word "luxury" probably conjures up immediate thoughts of Louis Vuitton and Lamborghinis and oceanside resorts (and these might be your idea of luxury), what I'm talking about are small, incremental upgrades to your own personal version of luxury and abundance. For instance, when you see your future self living the life you desire, what are they wearing? What sorts of things do they have in their home surrounding them? And could you possibly, gently gift yourself with one small token of that life? You don't have to rush out to get an entirely new wardrobe today; buy yourself one cashmere throw or a new pair of jeans that fit you well. I recently bought what I considered to be a very expensive throw for our couch just because it made me feel luxurious and gave the living room a boho vibe. My next-level self loved it!

As with everything, you can work with your abundance guide to explore what a doable baby-step into abundance might feel like, though I'm betting you have a few things right now that spring to mind. The cool thing about this process is that it usually doesn't take as much money as you think in order to create that feeling of abundance;

perhaps it's new flowers once per week or replacing that broken thing that's been driving you crazy. Whatever gives you feelings of luxury and abundance is the right thing to choose here; after all, our mission is to cultivate those feelings of abundance and joy, so that we can create even more abundance and joy, so whatever brings that into your life is golden!

Slightly Better Thoughts

As we've been doing, we're working on shifting your beliefs, programs, and energetic field around attracting what you desire into your life. One of the best ways to do it is gently find your way to different beliefs. It's difficult to go from "everything is shit" to "everything is awesome" in an instant, just as it's difficult to go from "I can never make money" to "I'm an abundant money goddess" in the next moment. One way to begin this gentle shift is to focus on a thought that feels just slightly better than the one you currently have about the world or a personal situation. For instance, if your current belief around your money situation is something like "there's never enough," you might choose to think something like, "Hey, at least we have money for a coffee. At least I have a roof. At least I have somewhere to get coffee."

The caveat here is that whatever you choose as a slightly better thought should be one that you can feel truly good about. If you currently aren't feeling that grateful about the big things you're "supposed to" feel grateful for, choose something else. Sometimes when I'm doing this work, I start with something as small as the pen I'm using to write with, the journal I'm writing in, or the birdsong outside—whatever I can truly feel as a source of gratitude and happiness in that current moment.

It's also important to celebrate small wins just as much as if they were the big things you desire. After all, when the universe sends you abundance, and you say, "That's not enough, universe. I have huge bills to pay, I need more than this one-dollar bill I found on the ground," you're blocking the energy of receiving. If you believe that everything is energy, it's helpful to remember that the energy of "that's not enough" is still an energy of lack. As you work with your abundance guides, you can ask them to help you to shift from those feelings of not-enough-ness back to abundance and gratitude. We can once again enter that space of allowing and opening up to receiving, letting go of the need to *know*.

You can let go of the need to know exactly how everything will play out by closing your eyes and asking your helping spirits for guidance. Just the single act of remembering that you are supported by the infinite wisdom of your helping spirits often helps to shift your energy very quickly—even if you're stressed out and annoyed. When you're feeling down, sad, lost, or distracted, tuning in to the guidance of your guides will help you to focus and realign and open up that flow of abundance.

Forgiveness, Anger, and Shame

Money is simply energy, and when we're blocking our energy in any way—including with thoughts of anger and resentment—we can block our flow. A healing process to release any feelings of anger or shame arising around people or situations, whether current or past, can be a powerful part of your abundance work. It feels good to release these energies and releasing them allows us to create even more feeling-good energy. (I mean, who wants to hold on to anger or shame, anyway?)

Creating abundance is really all about tuning into God consciousness, Universal energy, Source, the All-That-Is. When we're in that space and fully tapped into the power of love, there's simply no space for anger or bitterness toward others. You can always ask your helping spirits to show you places where you've held onto anger or shame and then gently release those feelings.

As with any forgiveness process, we're not condoning specific behavior, we're simply releasing our own anger and shame, which will once again allow our energy to flow freely.

JOURNEYING WORK

Heal Patterns of Not Feeling Deserving

- Please show me what's my responsibility to hold for the state of the world.
- Please show me how I can best help the world or particular situation.
- Please show me where I might be able to expand into luxury and abundance.
- Please show me possible steps to take into abundance.
- Where do I not recognize my deserving-ness in my life?
- What experiences have created a feeling of not-deserving or not-enough-ness?
- How can I be healed of these experiences? (This might be in multiple journeys.)
- What can I see or be shown about who is deserving of money and abundance in our world?

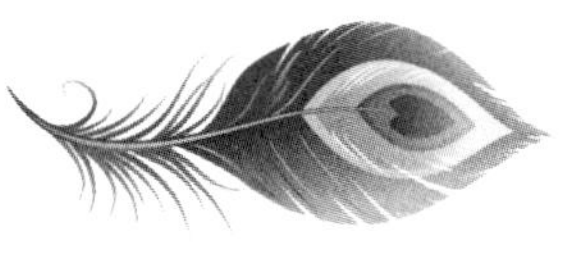

Chapter 14
Releasing the Need for Hard Work

Terry had already created a successful marketing business. However, when she wanted to do less of the hands-on work in her business and move into more coaching and strategy, she ran up against all sorts of problems: clients who demanded much more of her attention, virtual assistants who weren't delivering on their work, and so on.

When we dug into the beliefs she was holding onto, we discovered that "you have to work really hard in order to make money" was one of her strongest. If you're nodding along right now, you probably recognize this belief in yourself—most of us have some version of this belief. When we don't recognize and work to release the belief, we perpetuate patterns of self-sabotage when we try to go in a new direction or income level.

When you're being called in a new direction, there's most likely a belief present that says that if the new thing seems easier than what you're doing now, you're not "allowed" to pursue it. For instance, if you're a business owner who wants to grow your business without working as hard, you'll most likely find ways to self-sabotage the ease and flow you actually want to experience. This is normal! If you haven't looked at this belief system, you'll most likely find yourself creating other new tasks that will make the work feel just as hard; in other words, this is the mind-body's way of convincing itself that the patterns it has already seen are "true" in the world.

The same pattern-seeking could also happen in a traditional career. As soon as you start to expand into something that feels lighter or more enjoyable in your job, old beliefs about hard work will most likely arise and you'll find other areas that make your job just as hard. After all, it can't be easy, right? As with all the beliefs we're working with, the beliefs might have very old origins perhaps from past lives and most definitely from our ancestors and our childhood. Letting this belief go is most likely going to be an ongoing process. At every new level you're attempting to access— ease and flow and joy and yes, income—this belief will absolutely show up again, and it will do so by helping you find extra work so that your mind feels okay with extra income.

There are two ways out of this type of thinking:

1. Continue to work hard.
2. Take baby steps while releasing the belief that it has to be hard.

You might not want that first path, but you can still work hard or do things that still feel difficult. In fact, I wouldn't recommend shutting down the laptop and going to Belize for a month (unless you've already planned for that) because large and sudden shifts don't usually create the change we want to see; they're usually too hard on our nervous systems and our bodies instead try to move us back into stasis.

Don't quit the day job just yet! Instead, consider option two. And remember that as always, you'll have the help of your abundance guides to show you what might work best to release the belief, in addition to ongoing practices to keep you on the path of light, ease, and joy as you create more abundance.

Maybe you're thinking that yeah, it'd be really nice to quit the day job or even your business and *finally* do what lights you up. But then those voices rush in, saying, "No, I can't really do that. Nobody makes any money from that!" Please know that people absolutely will pay you to do the work you love—you simply have to believe it's possible.

The things you're dealing with in your real life are real. And at the same time, when you start to shift your beliefs about what's possible for you, you get to access a new level of possibility and abundance. What you'll have to step into as you follow your unique path is trust in the power of the universe. Trust in yourself. Trust in the power of your helping spirits. Trust that things can change. Without that hope, what else do we have?

Because you only have this one life, wouldn't you rather know that you have followed your path rather than listened to the voice that says "Will I really make money at it?" or "Will people actually pay me for this?"

JOURNEYING WORK
Release Beliefs about Having to Work Hard for Money

- Please show me times where abundance has shown up without me having to work for it.
- Please show me times in childhood where my belief about hard work was created.
- Please show me times I have created unnecessary work for myself.
- How can I best release this belief?

- What is necessary for me right now to let go of this belief in everyday life?
- What are some ongoing practices I can do to let go of working harder?
- Ask for a healing around this belief.
- Please show me times I have stepped out without knowing how it would look in the end.
- Please show me the times I have followed my own intuition and simply done the thing.
- If I truly *knew* what I could share right now, it would be …

Chapter 15
TAKING ACTIONS FOR ABUNDANCE

You don't need to take any action at all in order to access more abundance. Abundance already exists for all of us, so all we need ot do is call it into our reality. That said, most of us believe taking action is a requirement. Instead of working to shift this belief, you could take action toward your dreams. Please don't take that to mean that you need to run out and try to do a lot more stuff! Instead, discover and then take your aligned actions.

Aligned actions are not the same actions most of us believe we need to do. Most of us learned to operate within a highly masculine energy, which means that when it's time to do things to further our dreams, we usually go about it the wrong way: with urgency, haste, pressure, and relentless drive. And I want to be very clear: this isn't man-bashing. I love men. I'm talking about masculine energy, which isn't inherently negative. We need both the masculine and the feminine to create anything in our world: for birth to occur, the masculine and feminine are required. For a flower to bloom, there must be both stigma and stamens.

For both my fully-in-the-feminine-ease-and-flow friends as well as my high-powered types, action will speed up your abundance process. However, it's important that we take action from an aligned energy space so that we'll have to do a lot less than we might think.

Sometimes you feel like doing absolutely nothing. Usually when someone says they don't want to do anything at all and have ruled out obvious things such as a lack of rest, grief, or illness, that feeling might be one of two things:

1. Fear: What you're being asked to do is making you feel slightly uncomfortable. A good way to check on this is to look at the action you're being asked to take and see how your body is responding to it. You might be able to sense discomfort in your stomach, chest, or throat; all are indications that fear is holding you back.
2. Not actually feeling excited about what's being manifested: this one has come up for me often related to money goals. I'm not actually that interested in manifesting money, so I can't usually seem to take much action toward a money goal. However, I usually can take action toward

whatever I want the money to do for me, such as a cool retreat or vacation.

Of course, everything can also be created in an instant. You don't have to do difficult things in order to create the career or business you desire. The hard part, the real action is in shifting your energy into one of abundance, which is where most of us stop short. How many people take the time every morning to align with Source energy and the energy of abundance before they do anything else?

A great way to tune into the energy of abundance is to check in with your abundance guide and see what you might choose to do today to feel that abundance. You may receive answers such as:

- Getting out in nature
- Feeling thankful for the sun on your face
- Taking a nap
- Writing a poem
- Snuggling that baby or doggie

None of these suggestions mean spending hours in meditation or contemplating or journeying. Know that there is so much less "doing" required for your abundance. Your real work is in the moment-to-moment rearrangement of your thinking patterns. You must go from:

- "Not for me" to "Why not me?"
- "This hasn't happened for me so far" to "This hasn't happened yet . . . and now it is happening."
- "I don't see a way" to "There is always, always, always a way because I am always supported by the Divine."
- "I can't" to "I can do anything at all that I see in my imagination."

Shifting these thoughts is hard. Luckily, you can always ask you guides to help you to shift your thoughts, even if you're in the midst of a very stressful situation. Essentially, you can ask your guides to bring consciousness and acknowledgment to your problematic thoughts and then allow those thoughts to be released, as we've talked about in previous chapters. Once you find yourself feeling aligned and abundant, you might notice an action that springs to mind or you might not—nevertheless, the primary work is always in shifting your thoughts and energy.

And then there is deeper work involving the processing of deeper trauma, older or stored memories, and potentially ancestral memories, cords, and energy. This kind of work is best done with a healer, mentor, coach, therapist, or professional who offers help in this work. The modality is not important; what's most important in working with a healer is your sense of safety and trust with the practitioner.

Know that you're able to receive healing with many different modalities and ways of processing. Ideally, you should do this sort of work at least once per month. (Yes, that's an entirely arbitrary number. Perhaps you only need it once per year.) If you recognize that you have more thoughts than you know what to do with on your own, once per month might be a good start.

You will have to begin to navigate between the so-called real world, the world you can see with your eyes, and the one that you want to move into, the world that you can only imagine right now. It's helpful to recognize that you're already living in the world you created with your mind. Look around you. You became the person you are right now by simply envisioning this person. For instance, you first envisioned the type of job you have right now or the college you went to, and then it became reality. Everything that currently exists in your life you first saw in your mind.

When you have a desire for something different now, all you need to do is see the thing you desire in your mind and take action using the energy of "it's already here." There's no more to it than that. For instance, let's say your desire is to travel all over the world. You would begin by seeing the first place you want to visit in your mind. When you're feeling super excited about the vision, then ask: "What is the first step to move me there today?" As always, your guides can help you figure out what sorts of actions are most aligned to get you there. The hard part for our human brains is to actually take those actions.

JOURNEYING WORK

Determine Which Actions Are Aligned with Abundance

Connect with your abundance guide to see which actions will align you with more abundance. Consider asking the following questions:

- What are my aligned actions that will move me on the path toward my vision?
- What perspectives or shifts can I be shown about how easy it might be to access my desires?
- What have I not been seeing in terms of opportunities or ways of moving toward my dreams?

Chapter 16
Healing Ancestral Abundance Blocks

Nothing is created in a vacuum; our environment, community, and family or origin all contribute to our health and well-being. In our modern world, we tend to ignore these factors in favor of the Western model of treating symptoms instead of causes. Science and the study of epigenetics is now proving that the things that our grandparents experienced can carry on into our lifetimes. For instance, research on the grandchildren of those who survived the Dutch Hunger Winter shows that they are more predisposed to obesity, as if preparing for their own Hunger Winter. In short, the grandparents unwittingly changed their DNA while still alive and the trait was then passed on.

Our beliefs are also passed down through our genes and energetic fields. Our bodies are literally encoded with beliefs from our parents, grandparents, and great-grandparents. Science will probably prove this to be correct soon. In the meantime, you can play around with this idea of embodied beliefs and ask yourself whether it feels true for you. Tune in to one of your beliefs around money in your body, and then ask yourself if it feels older than you. When I do that work for myself, I can sense a ball of anxiety in my stomach that absolutely feels older than me and my parents. I come from a long line of "don't get too happy in case the bottom falls out" people on both sides of my family, an attitude that was absolutely passed down to me. I'm betting you have some of your own beliefs like this too.

We're not looking to blame or shame any family members, of course! All of our ancestral belief systems were created so that our ancestors could keep themselves and their children safe from harm. After all, better to be cautious than to risk the saber-toothed tigers out there! But there aren't any saber-toothed tigers around, so you're allowed to gently disentangle yourself from the beliefs and patterns that kept your ancestors safe. It's now okay to let go of the energy of these beliefs that have been stored in your body and energetic field.

Certainly, saber-toothed tigers weren't the only threats around—it was more likely that other members of society posed more danger to our ancestors. However, many of those societal restrictions also no longer need to hold sway.

For instance, women no longer have to have a husband in order to have a home or a checking account. And in most parts of the world, women no longer risk being burned at the stake for sharing their spiritual gifts.

Ultimately, whether these beliefs were passed down from your ancestors or not doesn't actually matter. Like all the work we're doing here, if it works for you and makes you feel better, great. And if not, discard it. Working with your guides around specific areas should be helpful and supportive—if it's not, don't do it!

JOURNEYING WORK

Heal Ancestral Money Beliefs and Patterns

Ask for a guide or benevolent ancestor to support you regarding healing ancestral belief patterns, and then allow that guide to show you the best ways to proceed. And remind yourself that you aren't the one doing the work—you are stepping back and allowing your helping spirits to do the work on your behalf. As they do so, you should feel entirely supported, not exhausted. You might still feel tired after journeying but not so depleted that you can't move or function.

Once you have connected with your abundance guide, you might request the following:

- If it is aligned with the light, please show me where this belief originated.
- If it is aligned with the light, please lovingly release this belief now.
- If it is aligned with the light, please show me how this belief was passed down through my ancestors.

Chapter 17
HEALING PAST-LIFE ABUNDANCE BLOCKS

Whether you believe in past lives or not, releasing energy patterns that don't serve you is always beneficial. And if the past life story or pattern that you're being shown in your journeys feels resonant, does it really even matter if it was truly a past life or is an energy pattern that you've been associated with in some way? For me, it doesn't. I just want to clear that and move on with my life!

If it feels scary to think about earning money or earning more, there's often a past life energy that can be explored and worked to release some of that fear. Many of my clients have experienced a past life in which they were burned at the stake, hanged, or stoned to death for doing the work that they chose to do in the world. For women especially, stepping into our goddess or priestess power could have resulted in death, and not just in the times of the witch burnings in the United States and Europe—it also happened to powerful African and Indigenous priestesses and shamans. One of my own past lives showed me a life in which I was part of a priestess community in ancient Greece and asked to share my body with men for money and the sake of the community. There were moments when I no longer felt comfortable doing that and was shunned as a result. What therefore shows up often for me is a fear of truly expanding into my goddess energy and magic for fear of losing the love of my community.

If hearing stories about past lives makes you skeptical, no worries. We can still heal with the stories and energies from past lives without having to believe in them at all because we all hold the collective energies of the cosmos in our bodies and energy fields. If it happened to one of us, it happened to all of us.

When you write a new ending to the past life with your helping spirits, you'll see the beliefs in your life shift faster. But as with all the work offered here, please don't think that there's something you *need* to heal before you can access whatever you choose to access in this lifetime. This work is meant to be supportive to your growth, not make you feel as though there's a past life you *must* examine in order to be abundant, for example. Nope—you get to be abundant right now. You also get to do this fun, powerful, and supportive work with your helping spirits.

You might find it's not helpful to continually delve into a past life once it's been healed in the journey. Although the information from a past life is cool and fun to learn about, it's easy to attach too much meaning to who we were in past lives, which can be another way for the ego to feel better about itself. At the end of the day, even if you were Jesus in a previous life, you're not Jesus in this lifetime. You still have to wake up and walk along the path of kindness and compassion and do the very human work of trying to be a better person every day.

JOURNEYING WORK

Heal Past-Life Money Blocks and Patterns

Connect to your abundance guide and ask if they are the guide who will support you in your past life work or if the work is best done with another guide or helping spirit. If the latter, ask if they can bring you to your past life guide.

Ask first for an attunement or healing with your past life guide. Remember that you're not doing this work—your helping spirits are going to do this work on your behalf. During your journey, you're allowed to simply witness whatever occurs without attaching any meaning to it.

Ask to be shown the following around a specific belief that you hold currently:

- "Please show me where this belief originated." (This would be the past life in which the belief was first created.)
- "Please show me how this belief might have echoed in this current life."
- "Please offer a healing around this past life."

This process doesn't need to be long and drawn out; you will probably receive flashes of insight into the past life as soon as you connect with your spirit guide or guides for past-life work. When you return, you are free to explore what you've been shown and any research into the time period if you like. However, know that this matter is already healed for you and that there's nothing further you have to do for the healing to happen.

Part 4

Ongoing Powerful Practices with Your Guides

Chapter 18

Healing the Earth

One of the largest responsibilities we have while following a sacred path is in honoring, respecting, and helping our earth to heal. No matter where you live, it's possible to create a deeper connection to the spirits of the land. This deep connection allows you to honor the land's original inhabitants—both human and in the unseen realms—and to be more attuned to the energy of the All-That-Is pervading all things on our planet and in our universe.

At the base of the Rocky Mountains are what's known as the Flat Irons, red sandstone ridges that jut upward from the city of Boulder and form an identifiable and picturesque backdrop for Instagram backgrounds. During the course of a program I took part in, I spent a lot of time hiking near the Flat Irons, taking every opportunity I could to get outside in the early mornings before our classes started at ten. It didn't hurt that I was coming from the east coast and was up early naturally. The magic of the Colorado landscape seeped into my bones, and as I took a walk near a lake at the base of the mountains on one of my last mornings there, I promised myself to always remember these times. We don't, though.

We forget the magic; we forget the call of the sacred amid our busy, normal lives until we're called back—sometimes gently, sometimes with a shout—to the forest and glade and desert. As my helping spirits continually remind me, the magic is not dependent upon where I live but instead where I find myself.

When you go on vacation, for instance, you might feel a sense of ease when you've established your connection to the land and honored the spirits in some way. It can be as simple as taking a walk barefoot and giving thanks for the ground beneath your feet, or a more elaborate ritual that names the spirits individually. At home, you might find it very nourishing to journey to the spirits of the land and representatives of the plant and animal kingdoms and ask for ways in which you can be supportive of the earth and her inhabitants. You might explore communing with the trees, plants, shrubs, flowers, insects, birds, and all other animals near you.

You might also ask to meet with devas, wood sprites, elves, gnomes, or fairies and ask for an emissary from each to greet you if you feel a particular affinity with them. There are many different realms to explore, even within the spaces of your home and the land around you.

One journey you might like to undertake while out in nature is simply sensing the energy of the forest or the trees. You might even like to journey to a specific tree and ask to be in connection with it. Simply ask whatever questions come to you, or ask how it feels or what it senses. What message does it have for you?

Working with the spirits of the land isn't just for your human benefit—it also helps the healing that needs to take place on our planet. You might even choose to journey to Mother Earth herself and ask how you can help with healing and upliftment. When we humans are more connected to nature, good things happen. We become more aware of what we are doing to harm the planet, and what we can do on our own little part of this world in order to help heal Mother Earth.

JOURNEYING WORK

Heal the Planet and Connect with the Land

There are many different guides you might feel called to work with related to healing the planet and connecting with the land. You might first undertake a short journey and ask to be shown where you can be of most benefit. If you already know that you wish to feel a deeper connection with a particular spirit of the land, you might undertake a short journey to be in connection with any of the following emissaries: spirits of the land or tree(s); ancestors of the land; fairies; elves; devas; Mother Earth; or an emissary from a particular kind of animal, tree, bush, stone, or plant near your home. Once you are in connection, you could ask or use the following as prompts:

- What is possible for me to see or do or know about the healing of the planet?
- Please show me how I have contributed to the misuse of our resources.
- Please show me followed by "how I can do my part" or "a commitment that I can make to help heal the earth."
- What sorts of offerings would the spirits of the land near me enjoy most?
- How can I most honor the spirits of the land where I live or am visiting?
- How can I be in deeper connection with the powerful beings that inhabit this land?
- How can I give thanks to the ancestors who previously inhabited this land?
- How can I make reparations for any harm done to this land? What is my responsibility in tending to this land?

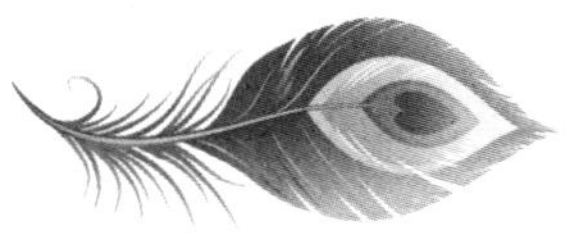

Chapter 19
Healing the Self and Others

When you connect to Source through the awesome power of your helping spirits, you're creating a state where your highest good can be shown to you. This state is already a part of the healing process, though you might also choose to explore specific practices for healing everything from physical pain to depression. As you heal yourself, you help heal the planet and the people around you. And as always, you can also help heal others in a more conscious way with the journeying practices you've learned.

Healing Physical Pain

The pain doesn't wake me up but as soon as I wake up, it's there: the radiating throbbing that extends from below my shoulder blades deep into the base of my skull. It comes and goes, this chronic pain. Sometimes I can go a couple of months before a flare-up, but a bad one will have me out of my normal self for two or even three days.

There's a small part of me that believes that I deserve this pain, that I've done awful things in my past that I need to be ashamed of; therefore, this pain is my burden. On a conscious level I understand this is completely ludicrous—no one on this earth deserves to be punished with chronic pain for mistakes they've made in the past. Yet although I know I don't "deserve" this chronic pain or need to be punished, the pain still exists and rears its ugly head. And I wish I could tell you I've figured it all out and completely healed everything with the aid of my helping spirits, but that isn't the case. However, I have received deep healings from my helping spirits for this pain on multiple occasions after which the pain fades to almost nothing each time. Sometimes the pain goes away during the journey itself or my spirit guides remind me of the things that help me the most, such as walking to unwind the muscles, stretching, or laying on a craniosacral pillow.

What my helping spirits have shared with me about physical pain is that it's always important to incorporate physical aspects of healing—the stretching, acupuncture, massage, chiropractic—whatever makes you feel good, along with continuing to receive healing on a soul level.

JOURNEYING WORK

Heal Your Pain

First, connect with an ally or helping spirit for healing. This ally might be specific to an aspect of healing (especially if you have chronic pain), or the helping spirit who shows up might be a more general healing ally. When you've established that connection, you could ask:

- How can I be in deeper connection with you?
- Where am I being led to explore my healing journey?
- What are some of the real-world tools I can use for my healing?
- Please share a healing with me now.
- What do I most need to know about my healing process?
- What is possible to be healed in this moment?

Helping Others Heal

If you're ready to help other people with the tools you've been learning here, that's awesome! We're simply the channel for the healing power of Source energy to be activated, not the ones doing the healing work itself. When we forget this and make it about ourselves, that's when we as healers run into trouble.

If you do choose to help others in a healing capacity, there are a few guidelines I urge you to consider and incorporate into your work.

1. Anyone we heal must be fully aware and have given us permission. By "fully aware," I mean the person must be conscious and able to make decisions. Though it might be possible to offer this work to someone when they're very sick and not aware of you, this is a gray area. In that specific instance, ask your helping spirits. The majority of the time we do healings, however, we're able to ask the person if they would like healing work and respect whatever answer is given. All people have free choice, and we don't want to force our healing on anyone.
2. When we're shown a recommendation from our helping spirits for the person, we can only offer it as such: a recommendation. We are not pushing our own answer on the person—and this includes children. Just because we think we know what's best for that person doesn't automatically mean that we *do*. We don't know why a person is experiencing what they're experiencing or what's "right" for them. We simply don't know all of the answers in the entire universe

and therefore cannot tell anyone what they "should" do. This naturally applies to more than healing work, but it needs to be explicitly stated here.

3. We're seeking open-ended guidance from both the person's helping spirits and our own. The way I assure this is through simply setting an intention at the beginning of the healing work to open up to healing guidance.
4. We are offering a beneficial and healing story to the one receiving the healing. Even if you're shown the causes or origins of a particular symptom, you might not always need to share it with your client if you don't believe it will be helpful or necessary. This also means that you might be shown things that could happen to a person in the future—if they're not beneficial or healing to your client, they might not need to be shared. This is another gray area, but you can work with your guides here to determine what might be most beneficial to share with the person.

Healing with Plant Medicine

People frequently ask me about plant medicine, so I want to be super clear: you can do this work without ever taking an entheogen or plant helper of any kind and still receive powerful insights and healing. There's absolutely a place for working with plant helpers, and indeed, there are theories that our spiritual evolution on this planet could have only come about with the help of plants. My point here is simply to offer the opinion that you aren't *required* to make use of plant medicine in order to have deep and powerful journeys or receive the amazing benefits of this work both for yourself and those you are helping. If you do feel called to working with ayahuasca, mushrooms, or any other plant medicine, reputable shamans or other trained facilitators can help you have a beautiful and powerful experience. And many Indigenous religions and traditions weave plant medicine into their work as a central component to connecting to the other realms. Again: plant medicine is never a requirement for having deep and beneficial experiences with your guides, as you've hopefully experienced already.

My own choice has been to continue to deepen into the work without the use of plant medicine, a personal choice that's predicated on my past. There were simply too many years in which I used drugs to help me escape my life; I wanted to escape being me with all my perceived faults. When I realized I could access the same sort of peace I'd once only been able to find through drugs simply by closing my eyes and journeying, it was a hell of a revelation. Mystical and powerful experiences were possible with just the beat of the drum! And by the time I began to explore journeying work, I already had children and simply wasn't interested in anything that would keep me from being fully aware or awake when around them. I didn't have to come back from or recover from spiritual work; I could just go back upstairs to my family and kids and still have a very normal day, even after an intense journey with my helping spirits.

Recreational drugs are not the same as ayahuasca, kambo, or other plant medicines, and I'm not comparing them here. Most people who choose to undergo a journey with an experienced plant medicine practitioner are not seeking a traditional "high"—and definitely won't be receiving one if they are! I simply haven't felt called to explore journeying through the lens of ayahuasca or any other hallucinatory plant helpers, but that's always a personal choice.

JOURNEYING WORK

Heal Others

Ask first for a specific guide to support you in offering your healing work to others. From there, you might choose to explore these questions:

- Ask for an attunement or healing with this guide.
- How can I be connected to you before offering healing?

- What is there to know about my healing work and medicine that I offer?
- How can I become more open to being the healing channel?
- What is there to know about protecting my energy during healing?
- What perspective or stance can I hold in order to allow for greater healing for others?

If you're interested in exploring plant medicine, one of the best ways to determine what is right for you is to ask your helping spirits.

- What is my relationship to the plant helpers of our planet right in this moment?
- Please show me ways plant helpers might be appropriate for me.
- Please show me how I can be in right accord with plant helpers.

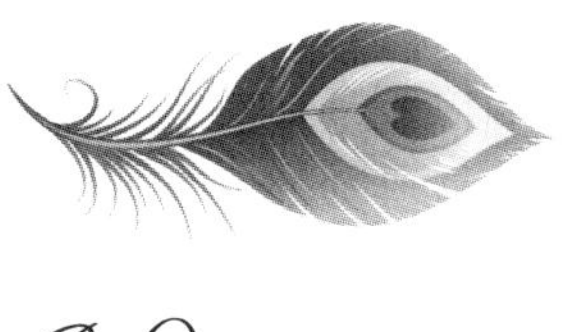

Chapter 20
HEALING RELATIONSHIPS

If there's something going wrong in a relationship whether with a partner, parent, friend, sibling, child, or colleague, we're usually waiting for the other person to change in some way. It's common for us to think, "If they would just see that..." or "If they would just stop doing..." or "They should really...." And if there's no one in your life like that, maybe there's a general perception about a group of people, like, say, people who voted for the opposing political party whom you also wish would change. "If they could just see how wrong they are!" But you already know you're never going to be able to change another person (let alone a political party) by forcing or even asking that they change their thinking, as much as you might want to. However, we can shift our own perspective. When you shift your energy around a certain topic, situation, or problem you might be having with another person or group of people, you might suddenly discover that the problem is not actually a problem.

The problem might magically take care of itself (or not) but either way, you'll have more acceptance around it.

Let's say your boss is not a nice person. You could take the problems you have with your boss into a conversation with your helping spirits and ask what can be shown or known around your situation. Your helping spirits might show you that your boss had a very sad upbringing, perhaps a parent who wasn't there. Or perhaps your helping spirits show you your boss as a baby with beautiful innocence. Or perhaps they show you your boss's soul and how much like your own it is. And then perhaps after this work with your guides, you're able to be kinder and more considerate to your boss, even if it isn't reciprocated. Perhaps your boss would then begin to soften and even come to apologize to you. Or perhaps that never happens, but you no longer get stressed about their behavior; your boss is simply who they are, and you eventually find a job that's more aligned with you, anyway. Or perhaps absolutely nothing changes at all but you simply accept your boss for who they are and realize that their behavior is not and never was about you. You are perfect and whole and complete, no matter what your boss does. Yeah, I realize that's much easier to say than to put into practice.

Here's another example that might seem a little lower-stakes than trying to make your boss into a cuddly teddy bear or totally transforming the political landscape. My husband kept lowering the blinds near our windowsill, crushing the plants beneath the blinds. I kept raising the blinds; wasn't it obvious that the plants were being squished? We went through this for three days, neither one of us voicing our opinions about this blind-raising-and-lowering, until the third day, when I yelled, "Can't you see you're killing the plants?" How could he not have seen it! His perspective was that he wanted to keep the summer sun out and keep the air conditioning costs down, saving us money. He was solving the problem he saw in front of him. He didn't wake up that morning and say, "I really want to annoy my wife today—I should mess with the blinds." And so it goes with most people (even those who cut you off in traffic); they're probably not trying to annoy you. Most people are kind and compassionate. They want to help you. They want to be kind to you. They're simply trying to solve the problems they see in front of them, even if that problem is just getting to work on time, which can occasionally mean that they're coming into conflict with what we're doing to solve our own problems. So how do you think my husband responded when I came at him with my anger? Not well—nobody responds well in the face of anger. But once I did some work with my helping spirits around my own anger and was able to fully see his perspective, I was able to approach the situation with humor, and I simply (wait for it...) moved the plants.

Please note that when we talk about releasing anger, that doesn't mean we condone or accept the other person's behavior. We're not forgiving them in a passive, "I choose to continue in this pattern" type of way. We can still make choices to end relationships or set up better boundaries if we need to. We can always choose to respond with kindness and compassion or walk away from the situation entirely. The choice is always up to us, even if it doesn't seem like we have a choice.

You can practice forgiveness of the self and others by reciting the Hawaiian Ho'Oponopono: "I'm sorry. Please forgive me. Thank you. I love you." It sounds simple but as you repeat the words over and over, you'll feel a shift in your energy.

Releasing Anger with Your Spirit Guides

When you're feeling angry or frustrated, your work is to be with your emotions no matter what they are and recognize what's yours and what's someone else's. Your spirit guides can be helpful in this process—you can call on them in the specific moment where you're annoyed or angry, creating a moment of conscious pause that many psychologists and somatic healers now recognize as so important in processing emotions.

Anger is often my first emotional response, so I've spent many hours working specifically with anger over the years. What it looks like for me is that I take the anger into a journey with my ally, Turtle, and Turtle holds up different aspects of what I'm angry about. Once we've identified an aspect and fully claimed it, Turtle very gently buries that aspect in the sand, transmuting the energy of the anger. We do this until I feel complete and the anger has been completely released. I learned this process when a very close friend told me how angry she was that I wasn't being supportive of her new relationship with a woman, and that I'd treated their relationship too casually. I was hurt, ashamed, angry, and saddened by her words. I took the entire incident into my process with Turtle and examined each aspect of the situation, which included things like my belief, "Everyone will think I'm an asshole now." I then held up each of my other thoughts around the situation, e.g., "What if she's right? What if I'm secretly not supportive of gay and queer relationships?" Turtle held each of these aspects up for me to see, and I really sat with each of these thoughts for a while. It was uncomfortable, but the awesome thing about helping spirits is that there is no judgment, only unconditional love. Turtle then showed me another aspect and another piece that I hadn't considered, and it was super freaking uncomfortable to sit with each one. This process isn't fun, but healing our relationships is perhaps the hardest work on the planet.

Eventually I got to a point where I could apologize with total sincerity to my friend for my missteps, and then I let the rest go. Whether she remained my friend or not wasn't up to me. Whether she told everyone else in our friend group I was a jerk also wasn't up to me. Whether she thought I was an asshole or not—again, not mine to own. I had to let it all go.

Luckily, this story has a happy ending: she and I are still friends, and I am much more aware of my unconscious beliefs and the words I choose to use with my gay and lesbian friends. That process was deeply informed by my journeying work with Turtle.

We often believe that if the other person would just change and become the person we want them to be, then we would no longer have a problem. However, no one changes their behavior simply because we ask them to, or at least they don't change for long. A person might initially do what has been asked of them out of fear or social pressure, but they won't feel good about it and will eventually revert to their old patterns. And people are also not motivated to change just because (and perhaps especially because) we've told them they're doing something wrong. They might initially accept our request, but they'll most likely react in anger or frustration or shut down completely. The same is true for our children.

People resist change. It's normal. We especially resist change if we sense we're being pushed into the changes by someone else. Imagine someone coming up to you and telling you that the way you're doing things is wrong in some way. What's your first reaction there? I know mine, and it contains a four-letter word.

Katie Byron writes in her book, *Loving What Is: Four Questions that Can Change Your Life*, about how she used to get super annoyed and angry at her kids for leaving their socks on the floor.[1] (I mean …) After her spiritual awakening, she came home and saw those same socks on the floor. This time around, however, she realized the socks weren't bothering her children at all. She was the only one bothered by the damn socks. So, she picked them up. Without saying a word. Without anger. Without any judgment of any kind.

Eventually, her children saw her picking the socks up. Knowing they weren't being judged at all, they began to pick up their own socks. So if something about another person is bothering us, we can't start the change process by asking them to change. Instead, we can just pick up the socks. Without judgment. See what happens.

1. Katie Byron, *Loving What Is: Four Questions That Can Change Your Life* (New York: Harmony Books, 2021), 28 .

If we want someone else to change, our best bet is to model the behavior we're hoping to see in the other person, that whole "be the change" idea. If you want more love from your spouse, model that. If you want more commitment from your children, model that instead of making the judgment that they're doing something wrong. Indeed, there's usually not even something wrong anyway, not in the conventional sense. After all, is there something inherently wrong with our children or spouses when they leave their socks on the floor? No, of course not. They're simply solving their own problem: they want to be rid of their socks in the most efficient way—which just happens to be right inside the doorway.

You may have a need to keep the house neat, which is understandable, but it still does not actually make it "wrong" for the kids to leave their socks on the floor. If the socks bother you and only you, choose if you want to pick them up today or leave them on the floor. After all, yelling at them about the socks hasn't changed their behavior.

The issue is bigger than just the socks, of course. Anywhere we're holding onto frustration and thinking things such as, "If they would *just* see that they're wrong," is a place we can expand our feelings of love and compassion. Perhaps there's a place in which we could extend even more kindness and compassion because we all know that countering violence with violence never works, even if the violence exists only in our thoughts toward another.

How do we begin to model extending that kindness? And how do we find the compassion we need in the moment? We can work with our guides to find different ways that will work for us as well and try out the following meditation.

MEDITATION FOR COMPASSION

(Adapted from Tibetan Buddhist Traditions)

See yourself as being connected to someone or something for which you feel unconditional love and joy when you think about; it could even be a place or a pet. See your heart energy extending to them. Really feel into the energy of that connection. Does it have a color as it extends from your heart? Can you strengthen that connection even more? Repeat silently, "May they be healthy. May they be loved. May they be at peace."

Next, feel that sense of unconditional love extending to someone for whom you feel completely neutral, perhaps a neighbor or a stranger. Send that same beam of unconditional love to them. Feel it enveloping them, strengthening the feeling, deepening into the feeling. Repeat silently, "May they be healthy. May they be loved. May they be at peace."

Now extend that same sense of love to someone with whom you have a difficult relationship or are experiencing frustration. See the same love going to them, even if it seems hard at first. Simply extend the energy from your heart center and allow it to wash over them. Repeat silently, "May they be healthy. May they be loved. May they be at peace."

At the end, bring your energy back to your heart center. Feel how enlivened and refreshed your heart energy feels. And then repeat silently for yourself, "May I be healthy. May I be loved. May I be at peace."

JOURNEYING WORK

Release Anger

Ask first which of your guides or helping spirits would be willing to help you with processing anger or frustration, and then choose one to two of the following questions that feel most resonant to explore in your journey with this guide:

- Where have I held the belief for another to be wrong?
- Where can I release resentment today?
- What would total compassion for others feel like in my body?

- How can I hold a perspective of compassion and kindness in the midst of difficult things and moments"
- What actual tools can I use while in a moment of anger or frustration with another human?
- Dear helping spirits, please show me a process for releasing anger or shame.
- Please show me where I hold onto anger or shame, and in which situations.
- Please show me how my anger or frustration with another person or situation might be blocking my flow.
- Where can I let go even more in this situation?
- How can I bring unconditional love to this situation or person?
- How can I bring unconditional love to myself here?
- How can I resolve this previous situation that causes me regret or sadness or shame?
- Ask for a healing around a previous situation.
- How can I release my worry over a particular situation or person?
- How can I see this person as fully healed?

Chapter 21
Releasing Energetic Cords

My client Betty is an incredibly bright, high-level manager at a large corporation, but she kept feeling like something was wrong or "off" in her life. As we started working together and exploring aspects of her life, a wellspring of grief rose up. Betty didn't know what the grief was about; only that she was incredibly sad. I journeyed for her and then guided her to have a conversation with the grief, wherein the grief was revealed to be sadness over not having a child by that point in her life. After performing a healing ceremony, it seemed there was one final piece to the puzzle: releasing of an energetic cord tying Betty to her mom's expectations for that child in her life, even though it wasn't something that Betty and her mother had even discussed.

Once I cut the cord between Betty and her mother, her grief lifted. She messaged me a few weeks later to say she was feeling more vibrant and alive than she had in a while and was able to process through the ending of her last relationship in a much healthier way.

Energetic cords are simply energy patterns or thoughtforms connected to other people, situations, and even old dreams in ways you might not want. Our energy is ours alone, so any time we've leaked energy to others, it's good to call that energy back by releasing the energetic cord. An energetic cord might be present if you've been experiencing a sense of sadness, frustration, anger, or any other unwanted emotion. There are many reasons you might be feeling sad, angry, or frustrated, just as there are an infinite number of paths to healing, so please don't believe that you can only heal if you release *every* cord. Don't think you are required to seek out these cords or else your life will be a complete mess unless they are released. Healing and releasing cords can be very helpful but the practice is absolutely not required.

If releasing cords feels helpful and beneficial to you, go for it. But if it adds more of a burden to your life, then let's find something that feels more healing for you.

In my own life, my helping spirits have offered up only two words to me lately when I tune in to messages around my business and my sacred path: "retreats" and "writing"—that's it. I've made a great living as a business coach for entrepreneurs, so the thought of giving up that business in order to only do retreats and write books is frankly terrifying. How will I make money? How will I find enough people who want to do retreats if I'm no longer offering individual coaching programs?

However, my abundance guides and the guide of my business remind me that I will always be supported financially as I pursue my soul work, and that I've always found the money to do the things I truly desire, each and every time. So why worry? Because I'm human, and because most of Western culture is built on the belief that money equals success or that money equals happiness. Even when we know these beliefs aren't true, we often believe them on a subconscious level. So when I start to think about reducing that income or letting go of what seems to be a sure thing, the old demons surfaced, mind gremlins that said things like, "But who will actually read your books?" and "But there's not enough money in that; just keep doing what you're doing!"

Your cords might also show up as beliefs or fears—you can release these with the same process you would use for any type of cord. When I worked to release cords to old dreams and ideas about my business, new opportunities began showing up in magical ways.

Your helping spirits are going to have the answers to all the questions you might have about cord cutting. Your helping spirits will also always show you the ways that you need to heal and even help others to heal in the way that's most aligned for you. Your personal path of healing might include cord-cutting or it might not; however you can always trust your guides to show you the most aligned path forward.

Releasing Cords to Parents, Spouses, Partners, and Children

Almost all of my clients have had some sort of cord to the people closest to them, and most especially to parents and their own children. Many of us were raised with patterns of guilt or need or requirements around love from our parents, and we unconsciously pass on these same patterns to our children. Those patterns or cords are normal! And it's also possible to now release those cords so that you no longer feel required to be anything other than your amazing self and love your children unconditionally.

Cord-cutting with people close to us doesn't mean that we no longer love the person; we can still be in relationship with anyone we choose. However, we no longer have to give our energy away, or to siphon away another's energy, either. A good way to explain corded energy is this: you can love someone, but if you rely on them for any sort of emotional fulfillment, there's probably a cord there. You might also have a cord if you notice you're too deeply involved in a child's or spouse's emotions, taking them on as your own. Another situation in which cords might be present is if you regularly do certain things to please those close to you, even when you no longer wish to do those things.

We want to step into a space of unconditional love, and releasing cords is one great way of doing that because it allows us to release the energy of conditions and requirements for our love. It is possible to have strong bonds with others that don't require siphoning your life energy to others or vice versa.

Releasing Cords to Old Dreams

One really powerful way to work with cords is to release the energy you might have associated with an old dream for your life. Perhaps you always thought you'd live in a specific location or have a certain kind of partner or vocation; even though it never came to be, you still feel a sense of yearning or restlessness when you think about it. When you release the energetic cord tying you to that old dream, you should feel a sense of lightness and acceptance of your current life. This doesn't mean that you have to give up on your dreams, but it's likely your new dreams are not the same as the ones your previous self held.

Releasing Cords to Old Lovers and Exes

Many of us have one or two old loves for whom we still feel a sense of yearning, regret, or even unfinished business.

Releasing the cords to this person or people can allow you to sink into the fullest state of joy for your current life and current partner. Like everything else, you aren't forgetting this person in any way; you'll still look back on memories with them with fondness if you choose, but you will no longer *also* feel that sense of regret when thinking about them. As you do cord work tying you to this person, it's likely you'll find that your old hurts, shames, and regrets around the relationship also appear during the process. It can be uncomfortable and make you sad or even angry to revisit these things, but allow your spirit guides to do the healing work here and show you each aspect of the old relationship to which your energy is still associated, and then gently release that energy.

You might find when you first start that you have many cords to release. Don't despair—it's totally normal. Once you've cleared some cords, you won't need to do it again very often. When you start to sense when you are being corded to another's energy, simply close your eyes and do a quick releasing process.

The way I think about cord-cutting is that if you find it helps you move forward into a better place in your life, it's beneficial. But if upon reading about cords, you start thinking, "but I have so many cords. How can I ever move or get rid of them all? If I don't get rid of them, I won't ever get over my childhood trauma," cord-cutting work might not be beneficial right now. Put down the book. Get outside. Hug your family members or your cat, call a therapist, and let go of the idea of needing to do any de-cording work for now.

JOURNEYING WORK

Release Energetic Cords

First, ask to be connected with a cord-cutting ally. Together, you might choose to explore the following:

- An attunement to your cord-cutting ally or guide
- A gentle process for releasing cords
- What most needs to be released today
- A quick and easy process to use throughout your day when you feel your energy flagging

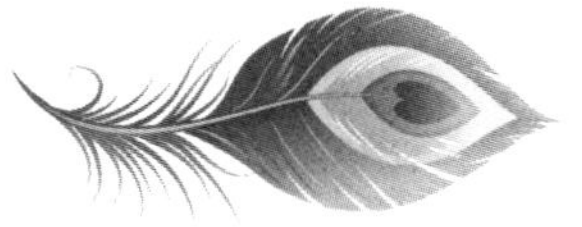

Conclusion

Eagle was one of my very first guides. She appeared to me during a session I had with a powerful shamanic healer. Tears ran down my face as she brought me to her nest high above the trees and showed me the beautiful eggs she had laid. Eagle was both a mother and a guide, and I was honored to be with her. In fact, I was so honored that I thought I had just "made it all up."

We're meant to question the nature of reality and our place in it. There's never an end to the quest for knowledge, and by "knowledge" I mean the deepest, oldest sense of the word: knowing we are human but also part of the Great Mystery.

What I can now see in hindsight is how each step of my journey has led me further down the path; the more I trusted in my guidance, the more amazing was the life I was able to create. When you truly open up to this mystical journey and the power of connecting to Source for all your answers, the journey truly does become easier.

The hardest part of this work will always be not allowing fear to take over that convinces you that what you've seen in your journeys isn't "real," "possible," or "logical." When we allow that fear to take over, we hold ourselves back from being in communion with Source and the universe. It's possible for every human on this planet to achieve that communion. Whether we choose to head down that path is up to us, but magic is possible in every moment.

And even while sitting at a traffic light or on your morning jog, you can listen to the messages from your helping spirits and hear what they have to say. This work is a continual dropping in, listening, tuning in, and allowing of the knowledge, even when it's scary or doesn't make sense at all.

Don't look to others to show you your unique pathway to this knowledge. There may be light posts or guides along the way, but your knowledge of this world and the worlds beyond will only come through direct revelation and experiencing of the powerful guidance you've been seeking.

You have more freedom than you've ever realized. You have more latitude to follow your dreams than you have ever even considered. Each step you take will put you on the path, provided you ask for that connection to Source. That's all that you need in order to determine your best steps forward.

You might still have questions about the nature of life, your soul, and the cosmos. You might choose to access your unique answers by tuning in to the energy of Source and your spirit guides with the following journeys.

JOURNEYING WORK

Answer Your Questions about the Soul, the Cosmos, and Reality

- Why are we born?
- How are our forms chosen?
- What level of control does our soul have for each incarnation?
- Are there past lives?
- Are there future lives?
- What can I be shown about multiple planes of existence and reality? Other dimensions, timelines, parallel universes?
- What can I be shown about the nature of reality?
- What does magic mean?
- What can I be shown about the nature of God/Source/Creative energy?
- What can I be shown about my own origin and how I chose to incarnate on this planet?

- What else can I be shown today about the nature of reality?
- Where have I held onto certain old forms of "reality" that can now be released?
- When do I most lose my connection to the Divine? When am I most aware of my connection to the Divine?
- How do I best cultivate that connection in daily life?
- What is a soul?
- How can I experience my soul?
- What is the highest offering of my soul right now?
- What pathways are opening for me?
- What does the soul's journey home look like?
- What does my soul look like?
- How can I help my soul to heal?
- What is left untended?

BIBLIOGRAPHY

Byron, Katie. *Loving What Is: Four Questions That Can Change Your Life*. New York: Harmony Books, 2021.

Duffield-Thomas, Denise. *Get Rich, Lucky Bitch! Release Your Money Blocks and Live a First-Class Life*. London: Hay House, 2018.

Hendricks, Gay. *The Big Leap: Conquer Your Hidden Fear and Take Life to the Next Level*. New York: HarperCollins, 2010.

Lumey, L. H., Aryeh D. Stein, Henry S. Kahn, Karin M. van der Pal-de Bruin, G. J. Blauw, Patricia A. Zybert, and Ezra S. Susser. "Cohort profile: the Dutch Hunger Winter families study." *International Journal of Epidemiology* 36(6): 1196–1204. 2007. https://doi.org/10.1093/ije/dym126.

Notes

Notes

Notes

To Write to the Author

If you wish to contact the author or would like more information about this book, please write to the author in care of Llewellyn Worldwide Ltd. and we will forward your request. Both the author and publisher appreciate hearing from you and learning of your enjoyment of this book and how it has helped you. Llewellyn Worldwide Ltd. cannot guarantee that every letter written to the author can be answered, but all will be forwarded. Please write to:

Erin Newman
℅ Llewellyn Worldwide
2143 Wooddale Drive
Woodbury, MN 55125-2989

Please enclose a self-addressed stamped envelope for reply, or $1.00 to cover costs. If outside the U.S.A., enclose an international postal reply coupon.

Many of Llewellyn's authors have websites with additional information and resources.

For more information, please visit our website at http: / / www.llewellyn.com.